THE LIFE CYCLE SERIES

CW00421344

Infancy

world of the newborn

Martin Richards

HARPER & ROW, PUBLISHERS
London   New York   Philadelphia
Hagerstown   San Francisco   Sydney

This book was devised and produced
by Multimedia Publications Inc

General Editor: *Dr. Leonard Kristal*
Prod Mgr/Art Dir/Design: *Bob Vari*
Picture Researcher: *Judy Kristal*

First published in Holland 1980 by
Multimedia Publications Inc

Published in Great Britain by
Harper & Row Ltd, 28 Tavistock Street London WC2E 7PN

British Library Cataloguing in Publication Data
Richards, Martin
    Infancy: world of the newborn
    References pg. 124–126
    Includes index

ISBN 00631 81223   cased
     00631 81231   paper

Colour origination: United Artists Ltd, Israel
Typeset by CCC, printed and bound in Great Britain by William Clowes
(Beccles) Limited, Beccles and London, England

Contents

*Though I am aware that nearly half all babies are girls,
I will follow convention and refer to them all as he, except
where my remarks apply specifically to girls.*

Birth and after

The term 'infancy' comes from the Latin, infantia, *which means an inability to speak. So, strictly speaking, infancy refers to the period of development from birth to the time when a baby begins to talk— usually during the second year of life. This book is about this earliest phase of childhood and it is written for the parents of infants by a parent who also happens to be a child psychologist. In writing it I am drawing both on my experiences with my own children and on research studies carried out by psychologists and others. My aim is to give a picture of babies growing up in our society—what they do and what their parents do with them. I hope this may provide you, as reader and parent, with a sort of commentary on your own life with your child, so that you may better see the many ways in which your baby is a totally unique individual and is yet at the same time surprisingly like all other babies.*

We live in a world where few of us have much to do with babies until we have our own. Families are small and children closely spaced; and it is fairly unusual for there to be a baby in a family by the time the older children reach adolescence. This means that when we have our own children we may not have any personal experience of caring for babies to draw on. Our own parents may live far away and we may not have friends with young children to turn to, so increasingly we use the professionals (family doctors, paediatricians, midwives, psychologists and health visitors) and their books as sources of information. This is not without its dangers. Professional people are as subject to fads and fashions as anybody else; and grandparents certainly do not have a monopoly of old wives' tales. I cannot claim to be any exception to this. However, by combining a parent's view with that of a professional I hope I can avoid the worst pitfalls. Adequately interpreted, psychological research can broaden our horizons as parents while our day-to-day lives with our children can prevent us from becoming too remote in our professional work.

One bias that some professionals have is that they see infancy almost entirely as a period of preparation for later life. They tend to concentrate on those aspects of babies' lives that have consequences for the future. My own bias runs in another direction. Of course the future is important; but I feel we must not forget the present. Infancy is an important time *in itself* for

'A flower of the next generation'—but his time 'in bud' is unique and important for him in this generation.

babies and their parents. It is a very brief period and for many people seems to pass all too quickly. I think we need to learn to enjoy it for what it is and not always be thinking of what we do with our babies in terms of the effects we think we may have on their future development.

For parents (and I think babies) infancy is a time of many varied emotions—of joy, love, fulfilment as well as frustration, anger and, all too often, exhaustion. Babies can be very demanding and ask of us things nobody may have asked us before. I hope that the picture I paint will be balanced—that I can reflect both the joys and the sorrows.[1]

The new person

We measure a life span—our age—from the moment of birth, which we see conventionally as our beginning. But of course most babies are already about 40 weeks old when they are born, and have already undergone considerable physical development in the uterus. Socially and psychologically a baby's life begins long before the delivery. This early life is in the form of the expectations, the hopes and fears that parents build up during the mother's pregnancy (and often long before that) as well as of the baby's own development.

Birth is then a crucial time, when these expectations and fantasies are replaced by the reality of a breathing, living baby. Many different feelings bubble up, often in a very confused way, at birth. Relief that the baby is all right and that labour is over; joy at what the parents have created for themselves—a new person, but one totally unlike themselves. There may also be disappointment or even disgust at the baby's appearance. A newborn may be wrinkled and red, streaked with blood from the delivery—altogether a first impression very different from the smiling chubby faces so familiar from the baby books. There can be fear, too, at the utter strangeness of a new baby, so recently part of the mother's body but now quite separate and apparently filled with mysterious needs and desires that may, at first, seem impossible to know or to meet. How can we ever cope with it all?

First days: home or hospital?
In industrialised countries almost all births take place in hospitals, where the mother is attended by midwives and doctors. This very recent change has important consequences for parents. A century ago our forebears were most likely to be born at home in their own parents' bed. A midwife or 'wise woman' was probably there with a female relative or friend to give help and assistance. Assuming all went well, a doctor was unlikely to be involved. Husbands were not often present as childbirth was seen to be very much a woman's business.

Since that time two major changes have occurred. Birth has become a primarily medical event and its place has shifted from the home to a hospital. This means that at a present-day delivery medical concerns predominate and parents' first contacts with their children are regulated by hospital routines and traditions. Such routines are subject to vigorous debate today, when many people feel that the so-called 'medicalisation' of childbirth has gone too far and that we are in danger of losing our sense of birth as a social and psychological event.[2]

Parents vary widely in their reactions to hospital. Some mothers welcome the way that in most hospitals everything is done for them and they do not have to take responsibility for anything. Others find this very disturbing and may resent the lack of control over what is happening to them and their babies and may long for the time when they will go home and can begin to get to know their new children in peace and quiet.

Our reaction to hospitals, as to so many things, will depend on our expectations and what we feel to be important about the event in which we are involved. But whatever our feelings about the birth, they *are* of importance, because they may well colour our initial reactions to the baby. Birth can be everything from the most ecstatic moment in the parents' lives to a nightmare from which recovery may take months.

At delivery the first concern of parents is usually whether the baby is all right or not. The doctor or midwife conducting the delivery will usually give the baby a quick examination before

Newborn babies are tested almost immediately for normality of reflexes— sucking, standing, 'walking' and gripping.

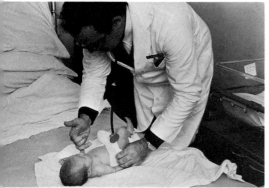
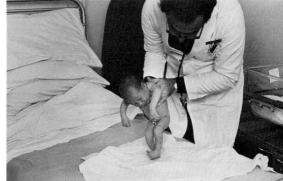
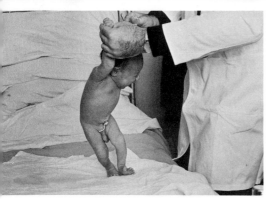
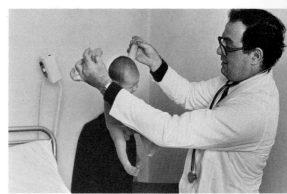

handing him to the mother and can generally reassure the patents; but a detailed examination is generally carried out a few days later, just before mother and baby go home from hospital. Once the parents know the baby is whole and well, they will want to know its sex—and this information will receive varying reactions (see Chapter 7).

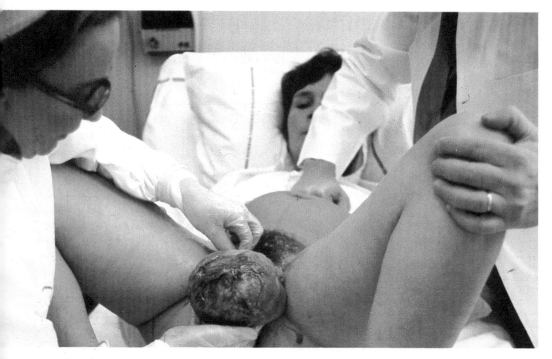

Strait is the gate that leads into this world as well as the one that leads out of it.

Assuming a normal delivery, a baby will generally cry briefly at birth and then settle into a fairly extended period of quiet wakefulness before going off to sleep. In most hospitals nowadays, as soon as the baby is delivered his face is wiped clean of any blood and he is loosely wrapped in a blanket and handed to the mother. Generally the father (or other companion) will be present and the two parents should be left in peace at least for an hour or two so that they can begin to get to know the baby. Often during this period the mother will put the baby to the breast; but this may have occurred even earlier, before the placenta has been delivered. The stimulation of the nipples by a sucking baby releases a hormone, *oxytocin*, which has the effect of intensifying the contractions of the uterus: sucking immediately after birth helps delivery of the placenta.

Unless the baby is depressed by pain-killing drugs (analgesics) that may have been given to the mother during labour, he will often suck vigorously for a time. Milk will not be present in the breasts yet, but the baby will receive *colostrum*. This is a clear, slightly sticky fluid which is thought to be important for the baby as it contains proteins which can transfer some immunity to infection from the mother to the baby. It has been shown that the earlier suckling is begun the easier it is to establish lactation and the longer the mother is likely to want to continue breastfeeding. Early sucking stimulates the production of milk in the breast and may well be important for the baby in 'fine-tuning' of the sucking actions.

Sucking involves a quite complicated set of movements and needs to be coordinated with both swallowing and breathing. The sucking pattern appears some weeks before birth—babies have been observed to suck their thumb in the uterus—but experience of sucking on a nipple or teat is required to give these patterned movements a final polish so that they become the highly effective means of obtaining food that they are. It seems probable that the sooner the baby gets this first practice after delivery the more effective the co-ordination of the movements will be. These matters are discussed in more detail in Chapter 2.

Meeting and exploring

Not surprisingly, parents usually explore their newborn babies during this period of first contact. Often they will unwrap the baby so that they can touch and stroke the whole body. Parents vary widely in the experiences they describe at this time: some report feeling quite detached and distant, interested in the baby as an intriguing object, while others experience an immediate overwhelming love and desire to hold and cuddle the baby.

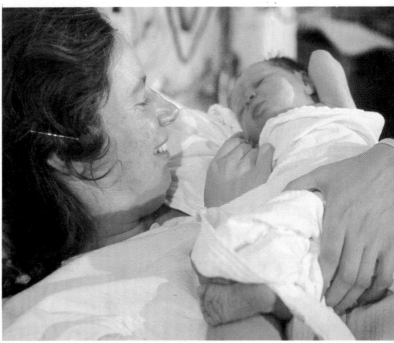

The beginning of a beautiful friendship?

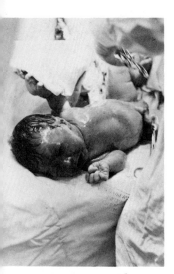

The first of the millions of breaths that fuel and constitute a lifetime.

Sometimes parents may begin to feel quite guilty if they do not experience this love at first sight but, in fact, surveys have shown that it is very common for days or weeks to pass before such feelings grow. Some recent surveys indicate that only about half of all women feel an immediate sense of love for their babies and if the labour and delivery have been complicated and analgesic drugs have been used, these feelings are more likely to be delayed. This is not surprising, since the commonly used drugs like *Pethidine* (*Meperidine*) often make people confused and feel out of control. It is very difficult to relate to anybody else in such a condition and especially hard to cope with the emotional upheaval of childbirth.

The first taking of breath

At birth the baby undergoes a sudden change in environment and has to make a very rapid transition from fetal life—in which all food and oxygen arrive via the umbilical cord from the mother—to that of a creature that is air breathing and must digest its own food. The first big shift is in the pattern of circulation, when the blood flow changes so that it passes through the lungs. At the same time, breathing movements begin and air passes in and out of the lungs. The period of quiet alertness after birth may represent a kind of recovery period from this first transition.

Newborns do not require food immediately after birth. If they have been well nourished in pregnancy they have ample fat supplies to last them a few days. During these first days a whole new series of physiological functions begins to operate as the baby takes over many of the excretory and other processes that have been performed by the mother's body while the baby was in the uterus.

Births 'not according to plan'

So far I have only considered normal deliveries. For a less fortunate minority, all may not go so well. A caesarian section may be necessary or the baby may be born with some condition that requires special treatment. Most such conditions are transient and after a few days or weeks all will be well. However, for a very small minority the baby may have a handicapping condition that will affect his future life. The parents of these children have much to contend with, for a handicapped child is the realisation of the worst fears of pregnancy. Much support and love is needed to help them live through the grief at the loss of the normal child they might have had. For many parents, indeed, the reaction to the birth of a handicapped child is very like the reaction to a stillbirth.[3]

Rates of caesarian delivery vary widely, but in Britain nearly 10 per cent of all babies are born this way. Though the use of local anaesthetics is increasing, most mothers are likely to have

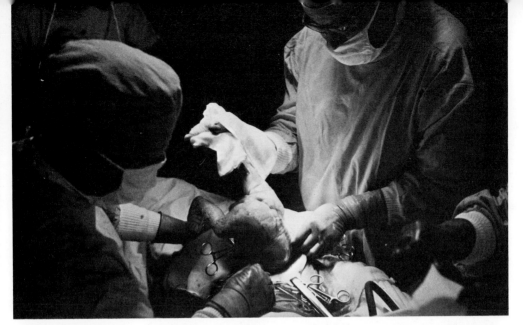

'...Ripp'd untimely from my mother's womb...'—but the gentleness and skills of modern caesarean deliveries leave mothers and babies with few scars.

a general anaesthetic and will therefore miss the birth itself. It may be some hours before they will see their babies and their period for getting to know their baby is complicated by the process of recovery from major abdominal surgery. Fathers (or other companions) have an especially important part to play at caesarian delivery. They can be present at the delivery and so greet the child; and they can tell the mother exactly what happened. Very often this can reduce the sense that some mothers have after a caesarian delivery, of having missed something.

When the development of caesarian babies is followed up, few differences are seen from normally delivered babies. It is sometimes thought that they might do even better than those born *via* the vagina because of not suffering the stress of being forced through a narrow birth canal—a force that often moulds the head of a baby into a rather pointed shape. However, it appears that the stress of vaginal birth to the baby has a physiological function and helps to stimulate the baby to breathe. Because of this, caesarian-delivered babies are sometimes somewhat slow to start breathing at birth and may require special resuscitation to start them going. The anaesthetics used for the operation also contribute to this delay.

Prematurity

If a baby is born prematurely (too soon), has grown more slowly than usual in pregnancy (small for dates) or has some medical problem, he may go to a Special Care Baby Unit (or 'Preemie Nursery)' for specialised attention. Here such babies are often nursed in incubators and may require a whole range of special techniques of nursing to ensure their survival and well being. In some countries nearly one in five of all babies are given some form of special nursing, so quite a large number of parents will begin their relationships with their babies in the very clinical atmosphere of the 'prem unit'.

Early separation and its effects

In recent years there have been several studies of the effects of early separation of parents and babies (either when a baby goes to a special care baby unit or simply because of very restrictive hospital routines) on the development of early social relations. This research (for example that of Marshall Klaus and John Kennell of Cleveland) has established that early separation *does* seem to create problems for some parents and that it may take several months for the effects to wear off.[4] Parents often report that they did not feel their child was their own until after they got him home and that they felt quite distant from the baby for some time after that. Others seem to be plagued by continuing feeding problems or by a baby that just does not seem to want to settle into any kind of routine.

'A giant leap for mankind . . .': infants as playmates . . .

It is not certain exactly why early separation should have these effects. One idea has been that there is a critical or sensitive period immediately after birth when a parent is particularly able to form a close relationship with the baby. If contact is denied or reduced at this time, it has been suggested, a much longer time than usual is needed to fall in love with a baby. Such critical periods are known in some animals: in goats, for example, if a kid is removed at birth and not immediately returned, the mother may never accept it. However, we have no direct evidence that the same sorts of processes occur in our own species.

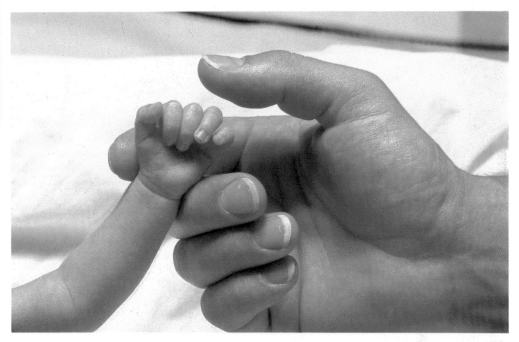

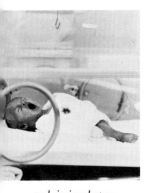

... as life-support systems ...

... and, in incubators, sometimes as remote as astronauts in space.

A more plausible idea is that people may feel rejected as parents if their babies are removed at birth. Many people already feel very anxious about whether they will turn out to be adequate parents. If a baby is taken to a special care baby unit, they may well accept that this is the best thing for the baby but still feel that they have, in effect, been treated as inadequate parents judged incapable of looking after their own baby. Often parents are given very limited scope for nursing or taking responsibility for their baby while he is in the special nursery and they may receive only minimal information about his progress. This may further increase their sense of a lack of self-confidence and at the same time lead them to feel that their baby is growing up a stranger to them.

Making the 'prem unit' more like home

Because of the results of the studies of the effects of early separation, routines in many special care units have been altered. Visiting is no longer restricted to certain hours and parents are encouraged to see their babies at any time of the day or night that they wish. Efforts are made to involve them as fully as possible in the care of their baby and to allow them to retain responsibility for his care. Breast-feeding seems particularly valuable in this situation as the mother can feel the dependence of her baby if he is taking her own milk. If the baby is too ill or immature to suck effectively he may be fed through a tube that passes directly into his stomach. In this case the mother has to express her milk manually and then she or the father feeds it to the baby through the tube. The experience of doing something for the baby makes an enormous difference to the parents' confidence.

There is also a biological reason why early direct contact between baby and parents is important. Our skins are covered by a rich flora of bacteria and yeasts. Technically these are infections but they are entirely harmless—indeed, these organisms probably serve several beneficial functions. A baby is born without this flora, but it is rapidly acquired by contact with adults. Normally, of course, the baby's first physical contacts will be with the mother and father and it will be from them that the skin flora comes. However, when early contact is prevented, the skin flora will be acquired from whoever handles the baby: if these people are hospital nurses and doctors there are dangers because they may be carrying disease-causing bacteria. Early contact with parents protects against such infections because once the skin is colonised it is more difficult for new kinds of bacteria to gain a foothold, so that damaging infection is prevented. It has been suggested that lack of opportunity for babies to be colonised by their parents' bacteria may be the reason why damaging infections have been such a problem in traditionally-run special care baby units.

How long in hospital?

After the first few hours, which, ideally at least, mother, baby and father (or other companion) will have spent together, both mother and baby are likely to want to sleep, while the father will begin telling family and friends about the birth. What happens from this point on will depend very much on how long mother and baby remain in hospital and on the particular kinds of routines in the hospital. Time spent in hospital after a normal delivery is being reduced in most countries from the ten days or a fortnight that were once common. In Britain, discharge after

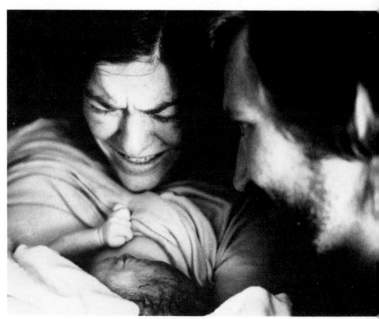

The nuclear family at its inception: all the relationships will be new hereafter.

14

48 hours is now often routine and not infrequent after only twelve hours. Though much may depend on circumstances at home and the parents' feelings about hospital care, there is a lot to be said for either very early discharge (within the first couple of days) or a week or more in hospital. The first allows the parents to begin working out their daily life with the baby from an early point without the need to adapt to hospital routines. But at the same time they will not receive the support hospital staff may offer during the initial process of adaptation to a new baby. Such support is usually available at home from family and friends as well as from district midwives or health visitors in the countries where these are available.

Some parents prefer to delay the transition from hospital to home until the first period of adaptation is complete—say about a week. This can allow a mother freedom to concentrate on her new baby undistracted by other demands at home. However, all too often what could be a period of peace and quiet before returning home is marred by frustration with hospital routines. Even today many hospitals feel it is necessary to regulate contact between newborns and their parents; to restrict feeding to set times, to allow babies at the mothers' sides for only a limited part of the day, to regulate visiting by relatives and friends and sometimes to prohibit all visiting by children including the baby's brothers and sisters. Ideal hospital organisation provides a system of choices so that the mother can decide for herself such things as whether she wants her baby at her bedside all the time (or she prefers him to sleep in a nursery for some of the day or night) and who should visit her and the baby and when. Such ideal conditions are still all too rarely found in hospitals. Where they are absent, hospital stays can be exhausting and demoralising and mothers may be only too pleased to return home at the earliest possible opportunity.

Breast-feeding

Around the fourth or fifth day after birth babies often go through a period when they are very restless and cry a good deal. This marks the time when they first become hungry. Up to this point they have been living on their own fat stores and do not need food; but by about the fourth day these fat stores are more or less exhausted and they become dependent on milk for their metabolic needs.

As one might expect natural selection has arranged things so that these first demands for food are met by the 'coming-in' of the breast milk. Before this time the breasts have been producing colostrum, but quite suddenly fill with milk. If a baby is given ample opportunity to feed at this time, crying and restlessness may be avoided as well as the engorgement of the breasts that may happen as the milk comes in. However, to do this feeds may

need to be very frequent for a day or so. Sometimes mothers are reluctant to do this for fear that they will set up a pattern of very frequent feeds. But even with total demand feeding the frequency of feeds soon begins to decline again.

Feeding troubles

Restriction of breast-feeding to every three or four hours—as is still found in some hospitals—leads to many problems at this time. The baby can be quite unsatisfied after such infrequent feeds and may cry a great deal, and the mother's breasts may become very engorged and painful. The engorgement may be enough to stretch the skin around the nipples so that they do not protrude enough for the baby to get a proper grip and he cannot suck properly. If this happens he gets hungrier and cries more while the mother may feel that she is quite unable to breast feed. The remedy is simple. The manual expression of a little milk relieves the pressure and then the baby can grip the nipples. Giving more frequent feeds usually avoids any recurrence.

Nature's way . . .

The blues

. . . and your baby is the best pathfinder.

This time is commonly one of emotional confusion for mothers. A brief period of depression or blues is a very common experience, especially for mothers in hospital. Quite inexplicably a mother may find herself crying and depressed. Or some rather trivial event which normally would not produce any reaction may assume great significance. A husband five minutes late at a hospital visit may appear to herald the end of a marriage or an off-hand comment by a nurse may be perceived as a total condemnation of the mother's capacity for childcare. Almost always these feelings soon pass, but at the time they can be very painful for the mother and those close to her. Their irrationality and apparent lack of explanation are themselves upsetting.

Nobody understands why such feelings are so common. It is often said that they are related to the hormonal changes in the body after the delivery of a baby. This may be so: hormonal changes do occur at this time; but no one has ever satisfactorily demonstrated which hormones are involved. It can also be seen in psychological terms as a reaction to the deep and profound emotions of childbirth and the transition from the potential parenthood of pregnancy to the actual situation of caring for a newborn baby.

Deep emotional experiences often leave people rather vulnerable so that events are perceived in exaggerated or distorted ways. Stress may add to this vulnerability and this could be the reason why these reactions are more common among women who are in hospital at this time. Coping with the strange institutional world of a hospital can be stressful, especially when an inexperienced mother also has a new baby to look after and her anxieties about her adequacy as a parent to deal with.

This latter point may explain why the so-called 'four-day blues' seem to be unrecognised in many non-industrialised societies. In these cultures parenthood is much more taken for granted than it is in the industrialised societies and the possibility that somebody will not be an adequate parent does not really arise. Moreover these societies usually have elaborate rituals and ceremonies which not only serve to acknowledge the new baby's membership of the community but also emphasise that child care is much more than an individual concern and responsibility. In such societies, parents are doing what many generations have done before them. Ways of treating children are not matters for debate and choice but are laid down by tradition and common consent. Concerns and anxieties which are more are less universal in our society—am I doing the right thing? Will I spoil him? Will I hurt him?—are largely absent. Our doubts and anxieties are a necessary price that we pay for a culture that incorporates the idea of individual freedom and responsibility; but it is a price paid largely by parents.

Introducing the new member

One consequence of the lack of ritual and tradition in our society is that parents have to find their own way of introducing the new baby to relatives and friends and, most important of all, to brothers and sisters. Cards, flowers and gifts are sent or brought to the hospital. Relatives and friends will want to see the new baby. Sometimes parents, especially mothers, may feel upset by all the attention if they feel it is going to the baby rather than to them. Mothers need a lot of support and reassurance after a delivery when their vulnerability makes them unusually sensitive to feelings of neglect. The situation was well described by Donald Winnicott, who always taught that just as a baby needs the comfort of a parent's arms, so too does the mother need holding— both literally and metaphorically.[5]

Parents may also feel competition for their newborns from the grandparents or other relatives and friends. Everybody may seem to want to hold the baby so that he gets no peace at all and the parents have little time with him themselves. In our culture birth is still an event with meaning in a wider family, like the annual festivals of Christmas, Thanksgiving and Seder Night. Couples without young children may become very accustomed to a private emotional life together and may be rather taken aback and resentful when the outside world suddenly intervenes once there is a baby to see and admire. At the time it is often hard for them to recognise how *their* baby also represents the next generation for the rest of the family. Their old feelings about parental control and direction may be aroused again if grandparents are too intrusive with their new grandchildren.

17

2 Growth and feeding

In industrialised societies, one of few details of a birth that people ask about and expect to be told is the weight of the baby. This, the sex and a name—if one has been already chosen—are the meagre facts that make up the public description of a newborn baby. (Under English law a birth must be registered within 28 days. But parents have a year in which to decide on a name for their child.) It seems that compared with the ways in which we might describe an adult we had just met for the first time, we have a very small vocabulary for describing babies. The social stereotype is that they all look the same anyway. But as the photographs below show this is far from the case. This lack of descriptions for babies emphasises how much we rely on people's actions, their social roles and the situations in which we meet them to describe their 'character' or 'personality'.

Weighing in

Because of the long interest in the weight of babies a good deal is known about the factors that may influence it and its consequences for later growth and development. The weight of a baby depends, basically, on its rate of growth during pregnancy and the length of pregnancy. Both these are very dependent on the mother's physique and health. Large healthy women tend to produce big babies, while women who themselves are short or have poor nutrition or ill health tend to have babies that grow less well and are more likely to be born too soon.

The range of birthweight is wide, as can be seen from the figure on page 20. Doctors draw an arbitrary line in this weight distribution at 2,500g (5½lb) and call all babies under this weight 'low birth weight' or premature. In Britain, about 7 per cent of all babies fall into this category.[1] This percentage is lower in countries like Sweden or the Netherlands which have higher overall standards of living and health, and higher in countries with poorer living standards or extensive poverty, like the United States or Italy. Or to put it another way, the more women in a population who are small, inadequately fed and of poor health, the greater the percentage of low birthweight babies. This

Lighter to carry than a week-end's shopping— but the weight of responsibility, love, joy and pain in that basket is incalculable.

category is an important one because low birthweight babies have a higher chance of suffering serious medical problems.

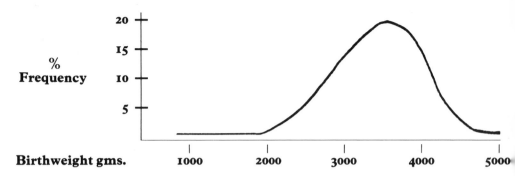

Perinatal mortality

Most countries collect statistics of what is called the perinatal mortality rate—the number of babies that die in the period around birth: the figures for selected countries are shown in the table below. This figure provides a very good overall indication of the general level of health and well-being in a country. If you break down these overall figures to see what babies die of, you find that there are two important factors—low birthweight and congenital malformation (errors in fetal development that give rise to physical deformities that are present at birth).[2] In Britain, as I have said, 7 per cent of all babies are of low birthweight; but this 7 per cent gives rise to no less than 70 per cent of all the babies that die around birth. To look at it the other way round, if a baby weighs more than 5½lb at birth and does not suffer from any serious malformation it is almost certain to survive. Only about one in 1,000 of these non-malformed, normal birthweight babies in Britain suffers from a problem serious enough to cause

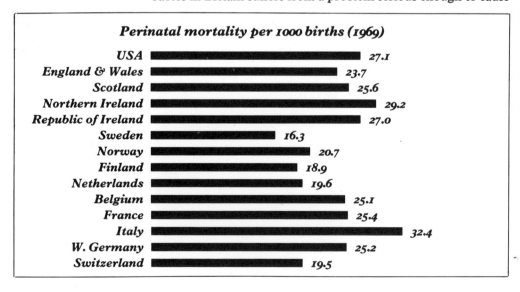

Perinatal mortality per 1000 births (1969)	
USA	27.1
England & Wales	23.7
Scotland	25.6
Northern Ireland	29.2
Republic of Ireland	27.0
Sweden	16.3
Norway	20.7
Finland	18.9
Netherlands	19.6
Belgium	25.1
France	25.4
Italy	32.4
W. Germany	25.2
Switzerland	19.5

death. So, although when compared with the remainder of the life cycle pregnancy and birth are relatively dangerous periods, the chances of dying are very small indeed provided that fetal development has proceeded normally and the baby has grown to a normal size.

Why is low birthweight such a potentially serious condition? Here we have to distinguish the two factors that separately or together may lead to low birthweight. First a baby may simply be born too soon. Clearly if the pregnancy ends before a baby grows to $5\frac{1}{2}$lb, even if growth is proceeding normally, the baby will be low birthweight. (Babies born at less than 40 weeks' gestation are called 'preterm'.) Secondly, the pregnancy may last the usual time but fetal growth is slowed so that after 40 weeks a baby has not achieved $5\frac{1}{2}$lb. These babies are called 'growth retarded' or 'small for dates'—small, that is, compared with what would be expected from the date of the mother's last menstrual period. The final possibility is that a baby is both preterm and growth retarded. This is quite common so that many preterm babies show a degree of growth retardation.

Preterm babies suffer problems because many processes in the body develop at specific times in pregnancy. For example, around 28 weeks the lungs develop a water repellant coating which enables a baby to clear them of fluid at birth and begin breathing. Without this, respiratory problems are common and can be very serious. Babies born before 30 weeks are likely to suffer from these respiratory problems. Growth retarded children have gone through the normal process of development and have passed the various fetal milestones but they suffer from a kind of starvation and have little fat or other resources to survive the upheaval of birth.

Modern pediatric methods have made a great deal of difference to the chances of survival and normal development for both preterm and growth retarded babies. Today it is possible for a baby weighing as little at 700g ($1\frac{1}{2}$lb) and as young as 26 weeks' gestation to survive with the help of these specialised techniques— a testimony to the extraordinary robustness and adaptability of the human fetus and infant.

For babies within the normal weight range, the most important determinant of their weight is their mother's size, not the father's. This principle was originally established in a rather dramatic experiment carried out with tiny Shetland ponies and large English carthorses. Crosses were carried out in each direction—with both Shetland mares and carthorse mares. In each case, the newborn foal was appropriately sized for the mother. As the foals grew up their size was more or less intermediate between their parents. This means that the much smaller foals from the Shetland mares caught up in growth with the carthorse foals.

This rule also applies to our children—their final height is likely to be around the average of their parents. Growth is influenced by diet and health. As these have improved over recent generations so has the height of adults. As long as things continue to improve it is likely that a child's adult height will be slightly above that of the average of his parents. These considerations mean that you cannot predict the final height of children from their size at birth, because birthweight is not influenced by the father—unlike adult height. Though there are some suggestions that a few growth retarded children grow into rather small adults, babies born too soon or too small usually catch up so that within a year or two most are the size you would expect from their parents provided that they are well fed and generally healthy in childhood. Growth gradually slows as a child gets older. It is faster during pregnancy than the first year and then slows progressively through childhood. After a renewed spurt at adolescence it soon slows completely.

Infant feeding

The human baby, unlike the adult, is adapted to a liquid diet of milk. Until very recent times this milk had to be provided by the baby's mother or another lactating woman. If it was not forthcoming the baby perished. Today artificial milks or *formulae* are available so that parents are faced with a choice of whether to feed their baby by breast or bottle. Much contradictory advice and opinion is offered on this subject so I will take a little space to describe the general features of each method before summarising some of the advantages and disadvantages of each.[3]

Breast-milk

Breast-milk is a very complicated mixture of fats, proteins, sugars, minerals and water that can provide all the food required by a baby for the first year or so of life. It is formed in the breast from substances which are circulating in the blood stream which are ultimately derived from what the mother herself eats and drinks. The formation of milk is controlled by a number of hormones, principally prolactin. These co-ordinate the development of the breasts with the growth of the fetus through pregnancy and ensure that *colostrum* is available at birth and milk a few days later. As milk is formed in the breast it flows into ducts and collects behind the nipples. When the nipples are stimulated, as when a baby begins to suck, the hormone *oxytocin* is released. This causes contractions of small muscle fibres in the breast which force the milk out through the small openings in the nipple. This is called the let-down reflex or draught. The reflex is easily conditional so that let-down may occur when a mother hears her baby crying or simply when she thinks about breast-feeding.

The baby's sucking

The let-down reflex on its own is not sufficient to empty the breast, the baby must also suck. Sucking involves a complex set of muscle movements which are coordinated with breathing and swallowing. At birth, indeed some weeks before, a baby is able to carry out these movements without apparently having to learn them. In fact, all the components of the movements occur in the uterus quite early in development and they are gradually 'assembled' into the complete pattern.

The basic suck, or semi vacuum, is produced by pulling down the lower jaw. As the cheeks are somewhat rigid, the space inside the mouth is increased. As the passage to the stomach and lungs are closed off at this point a suck is produced. The rigidity of the cheeks comes from slightly hardened pads which give a baby its characteristically fat-cheeked appearance. As well as sucking, the baby strips the nipple with its tongue while the nipple is pushed against the roof of the mouth in much the same motion as the fingers make when a cow is milked.

Emotional aspects

So far I have only considered breast feeding in physiological and mechanical terms; it does, of course, have important emotional and psychological aspects.[4] Most men see the breasts not as part of the body concerned with feeding babies but as sexual objects. As women in our culture learn from early childhood, breasts are an important part of their 'figure' which they need to attract and stimulate men. Feelings about the shape and size of her breasts contribute to a woman's sense of her own sexual attractiveness.

Breasts can be an important source of pleasure for adults, too—and even a store for nutrients!

They are usually a source of pleasure when kissed and touched in love-making. All of this makes the development of the breasts in pregnancy and their use to feed a baby confusing and disturbing to some women. The changes in shape in the body in pregnancy may upset a woman's sense of herself as a female being and may create anxieties about what her partner may feel.

23

At one time breastmilk was superior to bottled: but with modern formulae nobody should feel anxious about feeding in this way—and there is no difference in love.

Experience of breasts as sources of sexual pleasure may produce conflicting feelings when a baby is sucking at the breast. For some women these conflicts may be so strong that they decide to bottle feed their baby.

Part of the problem here is that our culture draws a strong line between the sexual feelings and love which are permissible between adults on the one hand and the love between parent and child on the other. Parent–child love is conventionally seen as being totally non-sexual. However, as most parents soon discover for themselves, there is a good deal of overlap between the two kinds of love. Many feelings experienced with other adults are experienced with children, too. However, little public acknowledgement is ever given to this. Parents sometimes become very guilty and anxious about these entirely commonplace feelings, which they may associate exclusively with adult sexuality, when they arise with their children. This can lead to cold and distant parental relations. Another way in which these same conflicts may surface is for a breast-feeding mother completely to immerse herself in the relationship with her child and to cut herself off from any close relationship with her partner, especially from sexual intercourse.

Breast *v* bottle

Much has been said and written about the importance of the close physical relationship of breast-feeding for the emotional development of children. However, repeated attempts to demonstrate this in research studies have failed. Though I think there is everything to be gained for a child from a close physical relationship with his parents this is neither ensured through breast-feeding nor precluded by bottle feeding. A breast-feeding mother can make feeding a time of closeness for her and her child, but this can happen at any time. The same is true for bottle feeding, which can be done with maximum distance or extreme closeness. Given this variability it is not too surprising that studies which have compared groups of breast-fed and bottle-fed children have failed to find any very striking differences.

Feeding patterns

If we compare our own culture with the remaining pre-agricultural or hunter-gatherer societies like the Kalahari San (Bushman) people or the Australian aborigines, or even with many agricultural and pastoral societies, the most obvious difference in parental relationships is how distant we appear to have become from our babies.[5] In these other societies babies are almost constantly with their mothers. During the day they may be carried by the mothers in slings so that a breast is more or less constantly available. Or they may be swaddled in a cradle or on a cradleboard within reach of the mother. At night babies usually share the mother's bed. Under these conditions babies do not

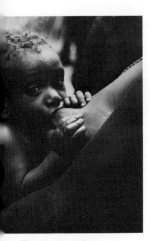

*Feeds at set times—
as still demanded
by some hospitals—
would not suit this baby,
who may suck as often
as every 20 minutes.*

have a number of set feeds during the day or night but suck in short bursts more or less round the clock. Observations of mothers in the Kalahari have shown that their babies suck at the breast about every 20 minutes.

Our society is geared to the idea of meals at set times and this is applied to babies. Being very adaptable, babies can accustom themselves to much more restricted feeds than would occur in a hunter-gatherer society, but there are limits to this. For most babies and mothers, feeding less frequently than every 3 hours, with one missed at night, makes the establishment of breast-feeding very difficult. Frequent feeding is especially important in the first week or two of lactation because the level of production of milk is to some extent set by the demand on the system. With too-infrequent feeds, the production of milk may never rise to the level required to sustain the very high growth rate of a young baby.

We do not really know if the more intermittent patterns of infant feeding characteristic of industrialised societies influence long-term development. It is certainly noticeable that in the last decade, as concern with and interest in the psychological aspects of infancy have grown, some parents have moved much nearer to the 'on-demand' systems of earlier societies and away from restricted and rigid feeding schedules. It has been suggested that there is a correspondence in a society between the pattern of infant feeding and the style of adult relationships.[6]

In societies like the San of the Kalahari, adults have a relatively small number of close and long-lasting relationships. Individual groups range from about ten to 30 people. Though some individuals move between groups, the total number of people that somebody is likely to come across in a life-time is probably less than two or three hundred. Our society is quite unlike this. Most of us meet several thousand people in a life-time and most of our relationships are brief and distant. At most workplaces emphasis is placed on keeping personal feelings and emotions out of our contacts with others. For many people the only close and long-lasting relationships are those between parents and children and between spouses. It has been argued that our intermittent patterning of infant feeding predisposes children towards this kind of adult social relationship.

Roughly speaking, kinds of infant feeding patterns and adult societies do seem to go together, but there are exceptions. My own guess is that our infant feeding patterns are more a *result* of our adult social world than in any sense a cause of it. I think children are predisposed towards the kinds of adult social relations that already exist in their society, but that this arises from patterns of social relationship in childhood which mirror those of adults, and not from patterns of infant feeding. Like most things to do with babies' lives the 'right' pattern of feeding is the one that the mother and baby work out between themselves to suit their own style of living. Parents should distrust *anyone*, however eminent, who is dogmatic on this subject. Parents are

25

almost certain to be disappointed if they set up any particular pattern of feeding in the expectation that it will produce a baby with a certain kind of temperament.

Breast-milk substitutes and 'formulae'

It is probable that ever since the time of the earliest human societies which had domestic animals attempts have been made to feed babies on the milk of cows, goats, sheep, mares and other mammals. Unless something was understood of the principles of sterilization it is likely that most attempts were unsuccessful. This is because, without the protective effect of human breast-milk, young babies are very susceptible to gut infections that give rise to diarrhoea and vomiting. As stale milk provides an ideal medium for the growth of bacteria the chances of infection will always be high. However, for the last 50 years or so special preparations of cows' milk in liquid or powder forms have been available for infant feeding in industrialised countries. As adequate means of protecting the milk from bacterial growth and for the cleaning of bottles exist, these provide a perfectly safe way of feeding a baby. The composition of milks from the various mammals varies quite widely depending on the diet of the mother, the growth rate of the young and the pattern of feeding. Seals, for example, have very concentrated milk with a high fat content. This allows the pup to build up an insulating layer of blubber very quickly. The more concentrated the milk the less often feeding takes place. Rabbits have relatively concentrated milk and feed their young once a day, leaving them hidden in a nest between feeds. At the other extreme, the milk of mice, monkeys and our own species is more dilute and is adapted to a pattern of frequent feeding. Cows' milk is more concentrated than human milk.

Over the years the composition of artificial baby milks has been changed so that they come to resemble human milk more closely. Though long experience has shown that they do provide an adequate food for a baby, they are not identical in make-up with human milk. Fierce arguments still continue about the importance or otherwise of these differences but it seems to be one of those problems that generate more heat than light. From the parents' point of view, there are perhaps only two points worth noting. First is the greater concentration of artificial feeds. This makes it possible to bottle-feed satisfactorily—at least from a nutritional point of view—four-hourly, which would be too widely spaced for breastfeeding. The other concerns the risks of infection (of which more below).

Here the risks are infinitesimal with a high standard of living in an industrialised country. But the situation among the poor and malnourished of the Third World is very different. There bottle-feeding is tantamount to a death sentence for many babies—hence the recent outcry against the promotional campaign in South America and Africa of European and American artificial milk producers. Unsuspecting parents in these countries spent their very small resources on baby milks in the belief that this was best for their babies whereas in fact it was the worst thing they could do. It would have been much better to breast-feed and use all the available reserves to supplement the mother's diet.

Some time in the first year, parents will begin to give solid foods to their baby. Like everything else to do with infant feeding this has tended to be another topic beset with controversy and rapidly-changing fashions. A few years ago in Britain some professional advice suggested that babies should begin on solid foods in the first couple of weeks after birth. Today the recommendation is for these to be started at 3 or 4 months. In

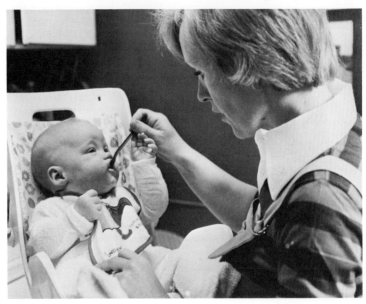

The first solid feed can be a battle or a mutual triumph: but there are good reasons for not trying it too early.

fact, there are very good nutritional and medical reasons for delaying the introduction of solids at least for 3 months. Breast-milk provides a perfectly adequate diet for a baby for the whole of the first year and the same is probably true for the artificial milks. Vitamins and iron supplements are often recommended for breast-fed babies. If a mother's diet is good, these are usually quite unnecessary. In fact, such supplements might be more appropriately given to the mother than the baby. The research on the iron requirements of babies illustrates a continuing tendency to believe that we can improve on breast-milk. Measurements showed that breast-milk contains much less iron than the modified cows' milk formulae (to which an iron supplement is added). On this basis, it was thought that extra iron was needed for optimal growth in breast-fed babies.

More recently, when iron measurements were done directly on babies, it was found that levels were much *higher* with breast-feeding. This paradox was resolved when the form in which the iron occurred in the two kinds of milk was examined. In breast milk much of the iron is bound in a special protein. This ensures that almost all the iron in the baby's digestive system is absorbed into the blood stream. In fact the system is so efficient that there was too little iron left in the alimentary canal to sustain bacteria that might otherwise have lived there—one of the reasons why breast milk provides a protection against infection. On the other hand, the much larger quantities of iron in bottle milk are in a form that is very poorly absorbed by the baby so that most of it passes straight through and is eliminated in the faeces.

A variety of special baby foods is available in the shops today. But as many parents find, these are expensive and may be much more trouble than giving a baby bits of food from the parents' own plates. Babies' chewing powers are a bit limited so it is wise to ensure that any food given is cut up fairly finely and does not contain bones etc. But it is not necessary to reduce everything to a purée as is sometimes recommended. To my palate at least, commercial baby foods are very tasteless. We have no good reason for thinking that the taste perception of infants is very different from that of adults or that babies are any less likely to enjoy a variety of interesting tastes. Indeed one reason for giving solid foods after 4 or 5 months is to provide babies with a range of taste experiences. They will not like everything and will quickly spit out things that do not give them pleasure. Favourite foods of babies I have known have included paté, kippers, curry and salami as well as a wide variety of fruits: they are certainly not limited to (and do not even necessarily include) the bland cereals to which so many children are condemned for their early months.

Breast-feeding: pros and cons

As will be clear from the discussion above, the relative advantages and disadvantages of breast-feeding to particular parents and children will vary a good deal with their social situation. In this section I will attempt to deal with the major points that may arise for people living in the industrialised countries of Europe and North America.

Convenience
Both breast-feeding and bottle-feeding have been described as 'the most convenient'. With breast-feeding, a constant source of clean milk is available for the baby provided that the mother is always close by and is able and willing to breast-feed. Bottle-feeding involves the purchase of milk formulae, bottles and sterilizing equipment, and the making up of bottles for each feed. The most obvious advantage is that anybody can feed the baby. Bottle-feeding probably costs more than breast-feeding but it must be remembered that the extra food required by a lactating woman (about 2,000 calories a day) is unlikely to be free. Bottle-feeds are usually warmed to around blood heat and extra equipment may be needed for this. However, warming feeds is not essential and some babies seem positively to prefer cold milk.

Breast-feeding is likely to involve more frequent feeds than bottle-feeding. And it does tie the mother to the baby: brief absences can be managed by the mother expressing milk by hand or with a breast pump and leaving this to be fed by bottle. Or a lactating friend can be a temporary wet nurse. It is certainly possible to give a baby an occasional bottle but not all will readily take to formulae (which may in any case destroy the immunological advantages of breast feeding: see below). If a mother returns to work outside the home, it is almost impossible to continue breast-feeding since almost no employers provide proper crêche facilities where a baby can be looked after and visited for feeding. When a father or other adult is to be the major caretaker breast-feeding is not usually possible.

Oh well . . . the breast-bottle debate does get rather boring at times!

The health of the baby

One of the most important advantages of breast-milk is that it gives the baby some immunity against infection, particularly those of the digestive tract. It does this in at least two ways. Protein molecules which make up part of the mother's own immune system are transferred directly to the baby in the milk. These are found in the highest concentration in the colostrum but they occur in milk too. Because milk is taken in much larger volumes than colostrum even the small concentrations in breast milk are significant for the baby. The other way in which breast-milk protects the baby is by making the alimentary canal a very hostile environment for bacteria. The very efficient way in which iron is absorbed from breast-milk means that not enough is left to provide nutrition for more than a very small number of bacteria. The chemical composition of breast-milk is such that the contents of the alimentary tract are relatively acid. This inhibits bacterial growth.

These protective processes mean that, for example, serious attacks of diarrhoea are much rarer in breast-fed babies. In countries with poverty and poor living conditions such infections kill large numbers of babies and young children and there breast-feeding can make the difference between life and death. In the industrialised world conditions are not so severe and at most all that breast-feeding may do is avoid an 'upset stomach'. Infrequently, however, outbreaks of infection do occur in hospitals: almost always the serious cases are bottle-fed babies.

A problem that can arise with some babies fed on formulae is that they become sensitive to cows' milk. Their immune systems react to some of the proteins in the milk passing through the wall of the gut into the blood stream. This permeability to 'foreign' proteins disappears after the first few weeks, but before that even a single formula feed can cause problems in the small minority of babies that are affected.

Other research has linked eczema and asthma to bottle feeding. The evidence is best for the first of these, for which it has been shown that the symptoms are relieved if affected children are put on a (cows') milk-free diet.

Breast-milk is often seen as a 'natural' and therefore wholesome food. But it must be remembered that its composition will vary with what the mother eats and that drugs and environmental contaminants that she takes in are likely to reach the baby. As many breast-feeding mothers have observed, the alcohol they drink also reaches the baby. In small quantities it makes an excellent sedative but, with too much, babies can get hung-over and may become very restless and fussy. Studies in the United States have demonstrated that most breast milk contains DDT, presumably derived from contaminated food. Levels are low and are thought to be harmless. Formulae can be contaminated in similar ways but it is much easier to impose adequate quality controls in a factory.

Drugs prescribed medically can pass to the baby via the milk and some can be dangerous. If you need to see a doctor make sure he knows if you are breast-feeding and if he prescribes a drug check with him that it is safe. Not all doctors are very aware of this problem and you should not assume that anything that is prescribed for you will be safe. *Get your doctor to check.*

When powdered milk is used to make up a bottle-feed it is very important that the instructions about dilution with water are followed carefully. Samples of bottle-milk made up by mothers and nurses in maternity hospitals in England have shown there is a strong tendency to put in too much powder on the principle that, if two scoopfuls are good for a baby, three must be even better. The problem is that milk contains salts and that to get rid of these through the kidneys the baby must have water. If the feed is overconcentrated there is not enough water to get rid of the excess salts and they accumulate in the body. If this process goes on too long it can have serious consequences for a baby. The first sign of *hypernatremia*, the technical name for the condition, is that the baby becomes fretful and cries a lot. This may be misinterpreted as hunger and the baby is given more over-concentrated food and so the problem gets worse. It is always worth remembering that babies, especially if bottle fed, may be thirsty as well as hungry. This is most likely if the weather is hot or the house is kept very warm. Most babies like fruit squashes and juice but even plain water will do.

The health of the mother

You are quite literally eating for two when you are breast-feeding. But provided that you eat well, health problems associated with breast-feeding are rare.

Some women worry about the possible effects of breast-feeding on the shape of their breasts. Most breasts sag in time but this is more a consequence of the growth in pregnancy than breast-feeding. Breast-feeding can help to remove some of the surplus fat that may have been deposited, especially around the hips, in pregnancy.

Many women complain of feeling tired, 'cow-like', and lacking in energy while breast-feeding. It is not clear whether this is an effect of breast-feeding itself or of all the new stresses and demands that come with a new baby. The hormone prolactin is at high levels as long as milk is being produced and it has been suggested that this may lead to reduced levels of activity and a reduction of sexual feelings; but direct evidence is lacking.

Psychological factors

From the discussion so far I hope that I have made it clear that no particular method of feeding is likely to have universal psychological advantages. Psychologically, the best method is that which best suits those immediately involved. Feeding is a central activity with a new baby, so it is hardly surprising that so much attention should be devoted to how people think it should be done. Young babies are very demanding and, in a society such as ours where many other kinds of demands are placed on adults, looking after them is very exhausting. The most fundamental disadvantage of breast-feeding is that it can only be done by a mother and is not something you can leave for a few days. Increasingly men are taking on more work in the home, including child care; and this can make breast-feeding much easier because it frees mothers from other responsibilities. It can also be a reason for not breast-feeding so that the direct care of the baby can be shared equally with or become the main responsibility of the father, if that is what suits the household. Parents will find many kinds of solutions to these problems and they should not be deterred from experimenting by any dogmatic belief in the overriding superiority of any particular method of infant feeding.

3   Sleeping and crying

Throughout the first year, the commonest complaint that parents have is that their baby wakes frequently and cries a lot. It is a worrying problem because it is hard for parents not to feel that they are doing something wrong which is the cause of the crying. And as their own sleep gets disturbed the worries are often compounded by exhaustion.

Perhaps the first point to establish is, how much do babies sleep? If parents have not had much contact with babies before they have their own, they often get the impression that newborns sleep more or less continuously through the day and night only waking briefly for feeds. In fact, babies are awake far more than this. On average, a newborn sleeps for about twelve hours to fourteen hours in each 24 and this drops to ten hours or less by the end of the first year. These are average figures; there is a good deal of variation and some babies will sleep more or less than this.

Pattern of sleeping

Sleep is not evenly distributed through the day and night. Within a week or so of birth a circadian (round about a day) pattern begins to develop so that sleep is most likely between midnight and 6 a.m.—a trend that most parents encourage!

The chart below shows the pattern of feeds for a fairly typical baby we studied in Cambridge. It was made up from a diary which the mother kept for us. By the end of the first ten days a clear pattern of night sleeping has emerged. This baby was born at home so hospital routines do not complicate the picture. Another feature that can be seen from the chart is the large number of feeds in the evening between 6 p.m. and midnight. Many babies are particularly fretful at this time.[1] No satisfactory explanation has been given for this 'evening colic'. It has been suggested that it is related to changes in composition in breast-milk through the day. As the protein content of the milk drops towards evening, it was thought that babies might get hungrier at the end of the day. However, we found that the pattern is as

'... *And just as we're getting to sleep tonight, she'll be wide awake.*'

common in bottle-fed babies as in those getting breast-milk. Another idea is that adults are more harassed in the evening and have less time for the baby. Certainly it can be a busy time, especially if it is a traditional household, where the husband expects a meal when he arrives home from work as well as other attention for himself. But again this does not give a very convincing explanation as the pattern is also seen in households where the father takes a major share in child care and the babies certainly do not always suffer any lack of adult attention at this time.

From a very early age babies are surprisingly sensitive to what is going on around them. Early evening is often the most social time in a household as it is then that all members are present. It is perhaps not too far-fetched to suggest that some 'evening colic' comes from a baby's sense of exclusion from this social activity. Often adults may try to organise things so that they have time for themselves in the evening and the baby is out of the way.

Finding a balance

It is very important for the adults to find time for themselves and not let every hour be dominated by the baby. However, given that babies are often wakeful in the evening it may be better not to aim for a 6 or 7 o'clock bedtime but to keep them up until 9 o'clock or so. If they are placed in an infant seat or anything that gives them a good view of the centre of activity, many babies are quite content to sit and watch people move around them. Daily routines are very much an individual matter and everybody needs to work out their own system making the best balance they can between the needs of all the household members.

The big sleep
Throughout infancy most children will sleep at least briefly during the day as well as at night. For many parents the length of night sleep is perhaps more important than the total amount of sleep in 24 hours. After all most adults are used to a routine where they have all their sleep in one go at night and, ideally at least, would want their baby to do the same. The table below shows the average length of the longest period of sleep for a group of babies we studied.

Mean length longest sleep bout (hours)

Age (weeks)	Babies who wake regularly during the night when a year old	Babies who regularly sleep through the night at one year	Babies
8	5·6	8·8	52
14	8·8	11·6	56
20	10·4	12·0	55
30	10·4	12·4	53

As can be seen there is a steady increase over the first year. For all these babies this longest period of sleep began at sometime between 6 p.m. and 6 a.m. but there was a great deal of variation between these limits.

In this study, the parents collected the information about sleep. Obviously they were not checking their babies every minute and the definition of sleep they used was that the baby remained in the cot and was not heard to cry. In fact, it is very likely that most of these babies were not asleep all the time they were recorded as being so. Sleep can be most accurately assessed by continuous recording of electrical activity of the brain (electro-encephalogram—EEG). Such studies have been done with babies, showing that sleep is a very complicated mixture of activities which occur in rhythmical cycles punctuated by 'awake' periods. These may occur about every two hours or so through the night.

Rapid eye movement

There are two types of sleeping, quiet or deep sleep and rapid eye movement (REM) sleep.[2] By watching a sleeping baby it is quite easy to see which of the two sleep states it is in. On falling asleep a baby (like an adult) first goes into quiet sleep. In quiet sleep breathing is regular and the body is still. A baby will look calm and peaceful. As a baby moves into REM sleep, his breathing becomes irregular and shallower. At times breathing will stop completely for a few seconds. This can be very frightening for parents who see it but it is quite normal. During REM sleep babies may twitch and move. Smiles, facial grimaces and sucking movements are common—as too are startles. Occasionally a baby may wake himself up with a startle, much as an adult may when falling off to sleep. If you watch a baby's eyes during REM sleep you can often see bursts of flickering movements of the eyeball. These are clearly visible through the eyelids.

Studies of adults have shown that dreaming occurs during REM sleep. People only report dreaming when they are woken up from REM sleep. Babies spend a much larger proportion of their sleep time in REM sleep—up to 70 per cent of all sleep. We

*Father taking
a supporting role.*

do not know why. Whether babies dream is a question we cannot answer as they are unable to tell us. All we can say is that the changes in electrical activity in their brains during REM sleep are very similar to those observed in adults who report dreaming. The essential feature of REM sleep is that the brain activity becomes less dependent on stimuli coming in from the outside and various inhibitory processes are reduced so that general levels of brain activity rise. In adults we have several reasons for thinking that REM sleep plays an important recuperative function and, as far as is known, the same applies to babies.

We can categorise a newborn's waking activity into three states but the boundaries are not quite so clear-cut as the two sleeping states. These are 'quiet alert' (eyes open, no large body movements), 'active' (eyes open, body movements) and 'crying'.

The habituation process

A baby has a certain amount of control over his state and is not simply driven from one to another by external events. Babies become quiet (move from active to quiet alert) when their

attention is caught by an interesting sound or object they can see. Unless especially interesting, new objects lose their novelty after a few minutes and the baby is likely to become more restless and to scan with his head and eyes for new things to look at. This gradual loss of apparent interest in things as they become familiar is known as *habituation*.[3] It is a very important process because it allows us to respond selectively to the world around us. If we responded equally to all things that we could see, feel and hear we would be completely overwhelmed by stimuli coming in. In fact, we are able to ignore the less interesting and unchanging elements in our world and so attend to things that are relevant. So as you read this you will not be attending to background noises—perhaps traffic outside, birds singing, voices in another room or touch sensations like the feel of your clothes. You can attend to these things by making a conscious effort. If there are changes in background sensations then the habituation process breaks down and we are conscious of them. For instance, we may be quite unconscious of the noise of an air conditioner until it stops.

Habituation saves us from being overwhelmed by the world we live in . . .

Most babies are capable of habituation right from birth. You can see this for yourself with a simple experiment. If a baby is awake sharp noises usually produce a startle response—a jerk of all or some of the limbs. If you make such a noise, say by flicking your fingers, the baby startles. But if you continue to make the noise regularly, say every ten or 15 seconds, the response will gradually decline and disappear. When it has disappeared to the flick of your fingers, it will return to another sound, showing that the effect is not simply due to tiredness. Similar experiments can be done with other sense modalities—sight, feel and taste.

The capacity to amuse oneself

As with adults, babies are not simply interested in novelty. If an object is well known and familiar and interesting it may retain attention. Experimenters have found that from a few weeks of age a baby will recognise familiar objects. If given a range of new and familiar objects to look at, a baby will usually look first at the novel objects but, unless these are especially interesting, will soon turn his attention to the familiar ones. In this way a baby begins to build up a picture of the world and his place in it.

After a few weeks a baby begins to be directly aware of the effect of his own actions on the physical (and we may assume social) world and this seems to hold especial interest. I will discuss this more thoroughly in Chapter 6, when I consider social games, but it is worth mentioning now the simplest form of the process, as it is probably a common way in which babies can regulate their own state: in everyday terms, it is the beginning of the capacity to amuse oneself.

. . . and so we need novelty.

A number of experiments have been done to demonstrate this

Give a sucker an even break! It is our own disapproval of 'easy pleasure' that makes us say thumbsucking is bad for babies: this is not how buck teeth are developed.

capacity. In one series babies were provided with foot panels which operated a switch when they were kicked. This was linked up to a mobile in the baby's line of sight which moved when the foot panel was operated by kicking. This set-up provided hours of amusement for babies who repeatedly kicked the panel to get the mobile moving. Now it might be thought that the baby does not necessarily make any connection between this kicking and the movement of the mobile, and provided that the mobile moves it is likely to be a continuing point of interest. Certainly mobiles that move quite independently of a baby's movement can keep attention for quite a long period.

Another experimental set-up showed that it was the fact that the baby caused the mobile to move that was important. Two babies were linked in tandem. Baby A had a foot panel which not only moved his own mobile but also another one over the cot of baby B. Baby B had a foot panel but this was not connected to either mobile. This experiment showed that baby A continued looking at his mobile for much longer than baby B. Then the babies were reversed so that baby B was controlling both mobiles. Now it was baby A who first lost interest in his mobile.

Few parents are going to build complicated toys like this for their children, but fortunately babies live in a world that is full of things that can be acted on in just the same way and, indeed, provide much more exciting possibilities than the simple feed-back loop of the kicking panel and mobile. Hands can be moved to hit rattles hanging in the cot, or to make shadows on its side. Kicking can move blankets. Hands can be felt as they touch parts of the body and explore. Kicking and other movements may shake the cot and this can produce interesting sounds.

Sucking is soothing

Another important way babies have of altering their own state is sucking. Sucking has a quieting effect. This is often seen towards the end of a feed when babies frequently fall asleep. But a baby does not have to be taking food for this to occur. Sucking a thumb, a fist, the teat of an empty bottle or a dummy (also accurately called a comforter or pacifier) can be equally effective. Babies often develop their own individual ways of sucking, some choosing their own hands, others apparently preferring a rubber teat. If the mother is breast-feeding on demand her nipples usually become the preferred pacifier. In previous generations, parents often tried to impose controls on a baby's sucking. Perhaps in an age of sexual repression parents were disturbed by the obvious sensual pleasure babies derive from sucking. Such fears became rationalised into statements like thumb-sucking causes misshaped teeth which, of course, have no foundation.

The exact kind of sucking a baby will use for self-quieting will depend on what is provided early on. In the absence of a suitable sucking object, some part of the hand is usually used. Once a pattern has developed it often remains unchanged for several years. My daughter chose a bottle as a sucking comfort-object. Originally when she was small she had fruit juice in a bottle: at

the age of three she always sucks on a bottle as she goes to sleep. It matters little whether there is anything in the bottle. Often if she stirs in the night you can hear her sucking on the bottle and during the day if she is tired or upset she still asks for a bottle. She has become very skilled at holding a bottle between her teeth leaving her hands free for other things.

Often babies choose a particular blanket or toy which they hold or stroke while comfort-sucking. Often a favourite blanket is reduced to a small shred of frayed material before it is finally abandoned by a toddler. As a baby I chose a towelling-covered penguin as my comfort-toy. By the time I was two the toy had disintegrated and all the stuffing had come out, despite frequent repairs, and I was left with a small piece of towelling. I continued to demand this when I slept. Perhaps it was this early experience that led to my life-long passion for bird-watching!

Donald Winnicott, the author of *The Child, the Family and the Outside World*, has called these comfort-toys 'transitional objects'. His claim was that they provided a symbolic transition between the physical presence of the mother and the mental image of her that the baby eventually builds to carry him through her absences. He may be right in putting such an emphasis on transitional objects as a source of comfort to babies when alone, at least for those babies that use them, but I am not so sure that these objects can be given as specific a symbolic meaning as standing for the mother. It is perhaps equally important to see them as objects belonging to the baby that are under his own control, almost as extensions of his own body.

Changing position

As well as these active ways a baby has of controlling his own state, there are several passive manipulations which can have quite dramatic effects. Changing posture has some influence. A baby is more likely to be awake and alert when upright than when lying down. This is well known to parents in many cultures but was relearnt the hard way by some psychologists who were investigating visual perception in babies. Using the first version of their apparatus in which the baby lay on his back with the stimulus objects suspended above the head, they found that babies frequently fell asleep before the tests were completed. However, when the baby was placed in a specially designed infant chair which supported the body in a more or less upright position, a much larger proportion of the test runs were completed successfully with the baby alert and awake throughout.

Rocking the cradle

Perhaps the most widely used means of calming a baby in our culture (beyond feeding) is through movement. When given a crying baby to hold, many adults find it is an almost automatic reaction to jog him up and down and to walk around. Until the

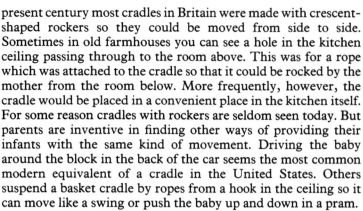

More comfortable, colourful and even 'technological'—but it is a cradleboard brought up to date for all that.

present century most cradles in Britain were made with crescent-shaped rockers so they could be moved from side to side. Sometimes in old farmhouses you can see a hole in the kitchen ceiling passing through to the room above. This was for a rope which was attached to the cradle so that it could be rocked by the mother from the room below. More frequently, however, the cradle would be placed in a convenient place in the kitchen itself. For some reason cradles with rockers are seldom seen today. But parents are inventive in finding other ways of providing their infants with the same kind of movement. Driving the baby around the block in the back of the car seems the most common modern equivalent of a cradle in the United States. Others suspend a basket cradle by ropes from a hook in the ceiling so it can move like a swing or push the baby up and down in a pram.

Given the effectiveness of the rocking cradle it is surprising that today they are seldom seen outside a museum or antique shop. I suspect that a small fortune awaits the manufacturer who copies one of these old designs, though I am afraid it is likely to be made of plastic rather than the oak that was traditional in parts of England.

Rhythmical sounds, as well as movements, are soothing for infants. The lullaby is probably as old as human infancy. Most have a slow rhythm which is similar to the frequency with which cradles are rocked.

It has been suggested that sounds of the same rhythm as heart-beats or recordings of heart-beats themselves are particularly effective in getting babies off to sleep. In several countries records of heart-beats designed for this purpose are sold to parents. The original idea was that when a baby was in the womb he would hear and become accustomed to his mother's heart-beat. After birth, it was suggested that a heart-beat would be soothing because it would remind the baby of a peaceful time before birth. Sadly, perhaps, researchers have shown that this rather romantic idea is not true. The rhythm of a heart-beat is no more effective than other rhythmical sounds of quite a wide frequency range. So the effect does not seem to be one specific to heart-beat sounds, but a more general one to rhythm.

Wrapped in swaddling clothes

Another calming technique that has more or less completely disappeared from industrialised societies is swaddling. Until the eighteenth century this was used in almost all societies in temperate regions and even today persists in a good number of societies—in the Middle East and among some American Indians for instance. The way it was done can be seen from many paintings of the Virgin and Child. Techniques varied a bit from place to place, but the basic principle is to wrap up the baby tightly so that the legs are together and the arms are held by the baby's side. In England this was usually done by wrapping cloth bands around the body.

Today people often react to pictures of swaddling by saying it is cruel. However, studies of its use in cultures where the

A slung baby is safe, comfortable and ready to its mother's hand— and breast—at all times.

Learning to walk . . .

. . . before you run.

tradition still persists do not support this. James Chisholm, an anthropologist from Rutgers University, has observed Navajo parents and their children.[4] Here, as in many swaddling cultures, a swaddled baby is strapped to a cradleboard which serves as a safe sitting or lying place. Babies are first put on a board a few days after birth and stay on it until they decide they want to sleep somewhere else—perhaps 10–18 months later. The popular myth that they spend all day and night on a board is quite untrue: they are removed for nappy changing, to be held and to kick and for general social play.

Cradleboards are not transport devices but are used so that the baby is always in close contact with the mother or whoever is looking after him. In a typical picture a Navajo baby is propped in a cradleboard at his mother's feet as she works at a loom.

Both laboratory experiments and field observations have shown that babies quieten when swaddled. Used in the way it is by Navajo parents, time when a baby might otherwise be fussing or crying is converted into either sleep or quiet alert state. Given that the cradleboard forms such a good vantage point for the baby, they have much more visual and vocal contact with other people than a typical European baby and about an equal amount of physical contact (out of the cradleboard). Careful follow-up studies of Navajo children have shown that development is perfectly normal; in fact, those on cradleboards seem to reach their 'motor milestones' (age of sitting, walking etc.) at slightly earlier ages than those who are not swaddled.

Used with care, swaddling, with or without a cradleboard, can be employed with babies in industrialised societies with advantage. By tightly wrapping a small baby in a sheet or blanket a fretful child can be helped into a peaceful sleep. For the technique to be effective it seems important that its use is started in the first few weeks of life. If it is begun when a child is several months old, they often fight against the restriction they are not used to. Swaddling with a thin sheet is very effective if a baby is restless in very hot weather, probably because it cuts down on body movement.

The other function of swaddling plus cradleboard which may be an advantage in our society is as a safe place for a baby in sight and sound of family members. A cradleboard can be propped or hung up where adults are working. In this way a baby gets much more social contact, because it is likely that without the cradleboard the baby would spend more time lying in a cot or pram alone. At the same time the adults are free to pursue household tasks. When my own daughter was small we placed hooks to hang her cradleboard at convenient places in the house—over the sink, above my desk—and both she and her parents enjoyed the freedom and contact it gave.

Infant seats can be used in similar ways but these do not have the advantage of the high proportion of quiet alert state that swaddling brings. Another holding device that has come into wide use is the baby bouncer. These can be hung up at any

41

suitable point in the house. If they are suspended so the baby's feet just touch the ground, they provide endless possibilities for self-induced movement as well as social contact.

Close contact

If you plot swaddling cultures on a map you find that, though it is used in hot regions, like the Middle East and New Mexico, it is not usual in the tropics. Here babies are usually carried on a sling on the mother's body. It seems probable that the reason why swaddling is not used is that the close wrapping in a hot and humid climate might make a baby rather prone to skin infections. Slings, like swaddling, have been experimented with by some parents in industrialised countries in recent years. Mostly they are used as transport devices. But some allow close contact of the baby with the adult's body. The movement of the baby as the adult moves has a marked calming effect on most babies.

In hot climates the baby in the sling is often in direct contact with the mother's body. If the baby is carried on the front he has more or less constant access to the breasts and can feed as he pleases. In other cultures he is carried on the back but slipped round to the front when he becomes restless so he can feed. As many observers have noted, you hear much less crying from babies in these culture: with true demand feeding crying is rare except where a baby is sick or hurt.

There is one interesting exception to what I have said about climate and the use of swaddling and slings. One might expect peoples who live in the cold Arctic regions to use swaddling. This is true for many Eskimo and Lapp groups though not all. In those groups that do not swaddle, small babies are kept inside the mother's anorak in direct skin to skin contact. There they are in much the same situation as a tropical baby in a sling. In fact, though the climates may seem so different, from the baby's point

Little burdens: and how to bear them.

of view they are probably quite similar. Inside a fur anorak the 'climate' is warm and humid—not unlike tropical Africa.

Fleecy lining
Another way of changing conditions for an unswaddled baby is to vary the texture of bed covers. Recently we have been trying out the effect of putting preterm babies in incubators on lambs' wool fleeces. Normally these babies are kept more or less naked on cotton sheets. Under these conditions babies show several signs of stress. We felt that this might be because they lacked skin contact. Lambs' wool seemed a good material because it is soft and a baby can sink into it so getting more skin contact than he would on the traditional hospital sheets. Comparisons showed that the change of bedding did indeed have quite marked effects on the babies. Crying and movements were reduced and growth rates increased. The babies appeared much less stressed and gave every sign of being happier.

Lamb skins are used at home for normal babies by a few parents. Often a piece of wool becomes the baby's comfort object. These fleeces are washable and can be obtained in most countries either with the original leather backing or with this replaced by woven cotton.

Baby and parents in the same bed
As living standards have risen, babies have been increasingly placed in rooms of their own. Often today a baby may spend a considerable proportion of the day and night in complete social isolation. The wider use of infant seats, baby bouncers and cradleboards has increased social contact for some babies but the new tradition of a separate room means isolation at night and often for part of the day too. Some parents have reduced this by having their babies sleep in their own beds. This is another point where conflicts of interest occur and everyone needs to make their own choices. Especially if a baby is being breast-fed, the advantages are obvious and it is clear that babies usually enjoy the physical contact. Fears about sexuality—both the baby witnessing its expression between the parents and fears aroused by physical contact with a baby—are in this case rationalised by statements about the dangers of lying on or smothering an infant. Certainly being laid on or smothered does appear as the cause of death for Victorian children, but there is little doubt that today we would classify these deaths as non-accidental injury or baby battering—they were a form of infanticide not accidents. Having talked to many parents who have regularly had their babies in their beds, I have only once heard of a potential accident. This was a case reported in a medical journal where a baby had become entangled in his mother's waist-length hair and had begun to be strangled before the parents woke and cut him free. The baby came to no serious harm. The moral is clear, but for those of us whose hair is shoulder length or shorter it is fair to say that a baby is safer in our beds than, for instance, on the living-room floor or indeed in a cot shut up in a room on his own.

Sleep problems

'*You thought I was asleep but I heard what you said and it's very hurtful ...*'

'*... and I can't fly and I didn't get X-ray vision and I've still got a wet nappy!*'

Surveys in Britain have indicated that more than 20 per cent of babies are regularly waking at night at their first birthday. For many households, this is a desperate situation. Exhausted and short-tempered parents can suffer an ever widening circle of problems that can have very serious consequences.

What can be done about sleep problems? Perhaps the first thing to do is to make out a daily time-table so you can see how much the baby is in fact sleeping. Often this will reveal that the total amount of sleep is not very different from the figures I gave earlier in the chapter. The question is partly *when* a baby sleeps. It may be possible for routines to be changed so a better compromise is reached between the parents' and baby's sleep periods. But the most crucial difference between 'sleep problem' and other babies is what a 'sleep problem' baby does when he wakes. Most babies wake at intervals in the night, but what characterises a 'sleep problem' baby is that he cries when he wakes and doesn't simply stir a bit and then go back to sleep. Our studies have shown that babies who regularly wake at night have usually been rather active and responsive babies throughout the first year. As newborns they tended to be rather jumpy and were fretful. These consistent and persistent behavioural differences mean that the problem is unlikely to have arisen through parental 'mishandling', a common professional assumption, but is due to a 'personality type' that has existed since birth. In fact, our investigations suggest that these babies are rather active as fetuses and that the pattern may be set up in mid-pregnancy, but further work is needed to confirm this.

A bored baby is a fretful baby

The usual advice given to parents whose babies continue to wake at night is to alter feeding schedules either to give more in the late evening, on the assumption that they wake from hunger, or to give less supposing that the problem is caused by 'colic'. But there are really no reasons for assuming that hunger has anything to do with the behaviour of these babies. Another tack is to prescribe a sedative drug. This does not often work as sedatives can have a contradictory alerting effect on young babies. Also many people feel that there may be dangers in the regular use of these drugs with young babies as their effects on an infant with a still-growing central nervous system may not be the same as on an adult. But the biggest objection to drug treatment is that it may not be getting at the right problem.

If we are right in thinking that the commonest problem is not a failure to sleep enough but more a question of what a baby does when he wakes up, it might be more productive to think of some of the techniques for calming a baby that I have mentioned. It may be possible to provide a baby with the means of self-quieting—by giving something suitable to suck on, for instance.

How every mother wants her child to look . . .

. . . and the lengths to which some of them will go to achieve it.

Or to provide a more interesting world in the cot by giving soft toys and suspending mobiles. One could say that a typical 'sleep problem' baby is one that has limited resources for self-control of states and self-amusement, so tends to become over-stimulated and fretful. If this is true we need to give the baby every possible opportunity for the development of these self-regulating capacities. But a problem here is that it seems much more difficult to change patterns once they have been established for some time and, of course, it is not usually until a pattern is well-established that parents recognise a 'sleep problem' and try to make changes.

Traditional remedies

We could say that the root of night waking lies with the kind of society we have constructed. Babies vary and there is no reason for thinking there were not always some infants who showed the behavioural features that characterise the night wakers. But we put enormous demands on babies and those who look after them. We expect babies to conform to daily time-tables, at least to some degree, and we expect their mothers to remain at home to look after them in a very isolated situation. In earlier times when work largely centred in and around the home, time-tables and living arrangements were probably more flexible. Households were a bit larger so that there were often siblings or servants around to share child care. Attitudes towards child care were probably not as coloured by anxiety and ambivalence as they are today, so that night crying could be ignored more easily and was not such a cause of parental worry and self-doubt. Traditional societies are much better than our own at passing on tried and tested techniques for child care. There was more direct contact with babies and children before marriage.

Certainly some of the remedies used a few centuries ago in Britain were not very effective but a few were possibly more use than modern equivalents. A case in point is the traditional treatment for colicky or fretful babies—alcohol. For minor stomach upsets my experience is that this is more effective than most things you can buy in a chemist's shop or are likely to have prescribed by a doctor. A patent medicine that is still sold in Britain for 'wind' is Gripe Water. Few parents realise that its major constituent is alcohol. It is an interesting comment on our sensibilities that parents who might well be shocked at the suggestion that they should give their baby a teaspoonful of sherry will happily make their babies quite tipsy on Gripe Water. To me, and I suspect to many babies, the taste of sherry is better than Gripe Water.

45

4 What can newborns do?

Quick on his feet ...

... and good with his hands ...

When we look at a baby we tend to concentrate on the features of his behaviour and appearance that foreshadow those of an adult. We welcome the first smile, the first word and the first steps because they mark a progression towards adult function. Much psychological research shares the same perspective. We compare an infant's behaviour with that of an adult and tend to emphasise those aspects which show the least difference. We are interested in infants as proto-adults. A film about infant behaviour, 'The Amazing Newborn', presents examples of ways in which infants are more capable than we used to think—more capable, basically meaning more adult-like. As adults, it is not too surprising that we see babies in this way, just as we consider chimpanzees 'clever' when they mimic human activities as in the zoo tea party. But in doing this we tend to distort the infant's world. In the same way the chimpanzees' tea party does not demonstrate the species' real skill which is to maintain a complex social life in the African forest.

Roughly speaking, the infant has two tasks: to survive as an infant and to develop into an adult. And the important point about this is that the capabilities required for life in infancy are not the same as those required as an adult. Perhaps this is made clearer by the example of animal species that have different body forms in the various stages of development. For instance, many insects hatch from an egg into a larva or caterpillar and on to a pupa or chrysalis before reaching the adult form of a moth, fly or butterfly. Each of these developmental stages has its own way of life to which it is adapted. Mosquitos begin life as eggs which may float on the surface of a pond. The larva is aquatic but the adult which eventually hatches out flies in the air. The food taken in each stage may be quite different. The caterpillar of the Common Cabbage White butterfly feeds on the leaves of cabbages, while the adult butterfly has a long tubular tongue through which it can suck nectar from flowers. For a species like this the capabilities of the caterpillar and its needs for survival are quite unlike those of the adult butterfly.

A human baby does not go through any sudden metamorphosis to reach adulthood but, nevertheless, the requirements for

. . . but every time
he opens his mouth
he puts his foot in it.

survival are not the same at all stages of growth. Diet, for instance, is quite different. A baby is adapted to live on a liquid diet of milk obtained by sucking, while adults take a wide variety of solid foods that require biting and chewing.

The years of dependence

The most obvious feature of an infant's world is his total and direct dependence on older members of the society for all his needs. Given certain basic resources, an adult can survive on a desert island but an infant or young child cannot. He requires a social world with adults prepared to care for him. From an evolutionary viewpoint, the long period of childhood dependence is a recent acquisition of the species and sets us apart from even our closest primate relatives, the great apes. For them infantile dependence is a much briefer proportion of the life span. Evolutionary biologists and anthropologists have suggested that the long dependence is the key to human evolution. This is because they see the dependence as providing a period in which to learn the social skills necessary for the maintenance and development of complex human social life and culture. The extended and close relationship of adult and child is, in effect, the cradle of culture. During infancy and childhood, learning and adaptation are much easier than in adulthood, so by extending childhood more can be learnt.

Familiarity breeds security both of which are of crucial importance to the growing child.

Our own situation can be contrasted with that of other mammals such as cats or dogs where behaviour is much more inflexible and fixed and the social skills that require learning can be picked up in a matter of weeks. In some species by increasing gestation time and so maturity at birth this time is even further reduced. A familiar example here is the guinea pig. Only a single pup is born, thus providing space in the uterus for the extended fetal development. At birth the guinea pig pup can run around and is even capable of almost the full repertoire of sexual behaviour. Species such as this have little opportunity for the passing on of skills from parent to child which is the hallmark of human development.

Language is one of the most notable human skills learnt during childhood dependence. A system of generative language, and the ability to use it appropriately for communication is unique to our own species. Without the years of dependence with a still-developing and plastic nervous system it would be impossible for such a complex system to be passed on from generation to generation—or indeed to have evolved in the first place. It is perhaps an odd thought that language and culture are the invention of babes in arms, not wise and experienced adults.

Teaching chimpanzees to use language

This is demonstrated by the experimental attempts to teach chimpanzees to use a language system. To teach them, a relationship analogous to that of parent and child is set up between psychologist and young chimp. At the same time the young chimp is carefully isolated from any chimpanzee culture. Under these artificially created conditions a primitive kind of language can be taught but the amount of learning is limited because effective teaching has to cease when a chimp reaches sexual maturity. This is partly because after this point it is not possible to sustain a dependent parent-child type relationship. Given that sexual maturity is reached quickly by human standards—within four to five years—the learning period is quite brief.

The evolutionary process by which a species extends the relative time spent in immature stages is called *neotony*. The classic zoological example of this is a curious Mexican animal called the axlotal. It is an amphibian like frogs or newts. In these species the tadpole stage, which has external gills and lives in water, changes into an adult which is air breathing and can live on land—like the familiar frog or toad. Sexual maturity is not reached until after the development of the adult form. What the axlotal has done is to short-circuit the process so that sexual maturity is reached during the tadpole stage. The adult form does not normally occur in nature at all.

Extended immaturity

Comparisons of growing body forms of our own species and that of the other great apes suggests that in our evolutionary past we have done the same trick as the axlotal. An adult human has several features, a large head relative to body size, for instance, that are characteristic of immature apes. But the real pay-off of the neotony process has been in behaviour, because it provides a long period of immaturity and an extension towards adulthood of the plastic nervous system of infancy that gives us, as a species, our capacities for learning and the handing on of tradition. With the development of this system culture, the ability to pass on knowledge through learning, becomes far more important than genetic changes in human evolution. In fact, what our genetic make-up allows is not the fixed and unlearnt patterns of behaviour which are characteristic of most animals, but it specifies the development of a system that is open to change through learning.

The giant step

The great importance of culture and learning rather than genetic change in human evolution is made plain in the ability of a baby to move from the stone age to industrialised society in a lifetime. The first human societies that made use of stone tools appeared about 500,000 years ago. But this evolution did not occur uniformly in all parts of the world so that even today there are cultures which represent an essentially stone age society. These groups live by hunting and gathering fruits and roots, not fixed agriculture, though increasingly, of course, they are being drastically altered by their contacts with industrialised society. People who have made the transition from these hunting and gathering societies to our own industrialised world show that it is quite possible for an individual to make the transition in a lifetime, especially if the move occurs in childhood. These cases demonstrate that the evolution from the simplest human social groups to our present-day societies does not involve biological change, but is the result of cultural developments that are passed on from generation to generation, especially by parents and siblings in early childhood.

So when we come to ask what babies can do it is useful to have two kinds of questions in mind—how is a baby's behaviour adapted to its life as a dependent infant and how far can we identify the processes that allow the development of adult function?

An effective system to provide care for dependent young requires adaptation from both sides: not only must the infant be fitted for such a life but others must be prepared to provide the necessary caretaking. Some of the early ethologists like Konrad Lorenz have talked of the attractive features of babies—the rounded face, large eyes and so on—and have seen these as adaptations to successful babyhood. So they may be, but only if caretakers find them attractive. Such a concentration on the special features of babies leaves out a vital feature of the human system; the adaptation of parents and others so that they are willing to look after mewling and puking children. The development of human society must have involved the creation of a social world which encouraged parents to devote a large proportion of their adult energies to childcare.

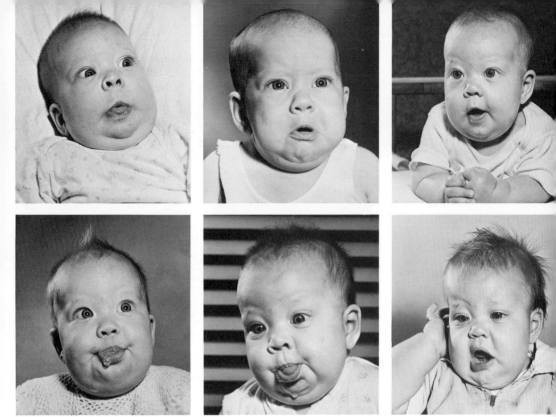

Behaviour patterns

The baby face develops: Some people believe that such expressions are Nature's way of making sure the baby is noticed: and if you are saying 'Aaah,' they are most probably quite right.

The most influential ethological writer on parent–child relationships has been John Bowlby.[1] He, like the other ethologists, took the caretakers' responses as given and developed a theory of social relations, attachment theory, in terms of the infant's behaviour. Though his theory is now seen as seriously deficient and oversimplified it still has a few supporters. Bowlby suggested that there were five aspects of infant behaviour which brought the mother (the theory totally ignores caretakers other than natural mothers or mother figures) to the baby and held her attention. This close proximity leads to the growth of the social relationship. The aspects of infant behaviour which Bowlby picked on perhaps as much reflected ethological work with monkey species as observation of human babies. Where human observations were involved they tended to be rather ethnocentric. His list of those special behaviour patterns was clinging, sucking, crying, smiling and following.

Though newborns are well able to grasp objects placed in their hands, clinging in our own species (unlike the monkeys and apes) is not a part of an infant's repertoire. It is not until well into the second half of the first year that infants are able to move independently and adjust the distance between themselves and others (again unlike monkeys and apes). So following too, which is important in many animal species, only becomes central after the point when the human infant has established its primary relationships. Sucking plays an obvious role in infant feeding but its place in the formation of social relationships is variable. Many infants form close ties with people who never feed them so that sucking is clearly not essential. Smiling is important in social relations, while crying plays a variable role depending on the culture. Where babies are generally kept away from caretakers for much of the day and night, as in the industrialised societies, crying is very important as a signal to caretakers. But where babies are always in close proximity and are fed more or less on demand, its role is mostly as a signal that a baby is in danger and needs immediate help.

Exploring his own dependency
Bowlby's formulations did provide a stimulus for the study of early social relationships but this later research has given us a rather different framework. Instead of seeing the infant's relationships as being based on a small number of specific behaviour patterns, the emphasis is now on the variety of behaviour patterns that can be involved. Variety exists not only because babies live quite different lives in different cultures (compare an African baby that spends its days carried on a sling and its nights in the mother's bed with a typical British or American infant), but because each baby and his caretakers to some extent work out their private system of communication. What is general is the infant's responsiveness to social companions. Within a few weeks of birth he can signal his interest in social interaction by his attention and smiles, and can break it off by turning away his head or simply closing his eyes. Above all, an infant is adapted to exploit his situation of dependency by developing a complex social life and a communication system.

Rising and falling body temperature

It is necessary to wrap the newborn 'present' well, thus ensuring no heat loss.

Dependency means that an infant can delay some aspects of development because he can rely on his needs being met by others. For example, the effective regulation of temperature is

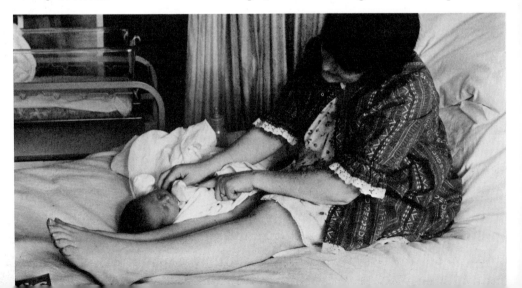

not fully present at birth. Shivering (to raise body temperature) and sweating (to reduce it) are not fully effective and the infant is, of course. quite unable to adjust the amount of his clothing. Without clothing in an environment cooler than blood temperature an infant cools quite quickly, especially because as compared with an adult he has a high ratio of body surface to weight. If the temperature rises above 37°C (98·4°F), his body temperature will rise. Normally caretakers clothe a baby so his temperature remains at normal whatever outside conditions. The risk of rapid heat loss is the reason why it is important to wrap a baby after delivery or keep him in close body contact. As the baby is wet at birth and cools with evaporation, even at very high temperatures the body temperature can fall unless precautions are taken. Overheating is usually less of a problem, but heat stroke has been recorded when babies are left in cars in the sun or simply overdressed. Recently a four-month-old was admitted to an English hospital with serious heat stroke. He had been put to bed on a warm and humid September night wearing a nappy, rubber pants, a sleeping suit, and a jersey and covered with four well-tucked-in blankets. Under these conditions body temperature can rise (very dangerously) above 40°C (104°F).

Infants will submit to being 'toilet trained'; but in response to parental ideas of what is clean rather than their own needs. And some psychologists think it has bad after-effects.

Control of elimination is another ability which an infant can afford not to develop for the first couple of years despite what parents might sometimes feel about this. Such signs of immaturity should not lead us to see babies as being incapable of any skilled movements or actions. It is simply that development is selective and provides what is needed. So we can contrast the relative immaturity of bowel and bladder control and locomotor movements (crawling and walking) with the maturity of sucking and the coordination of head and eye movements. I have already

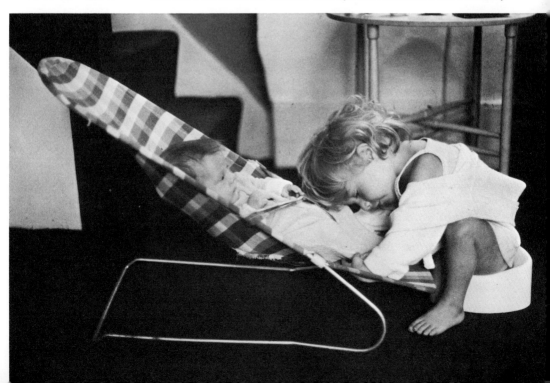

mentioned that a newborn is capable of sucking, and coordinating this with swallowing and breathing. The utility of this is obvious. He can also signal his hunger through crying and body movements and can turn his head to locate a nipple and grasp it in his lips. This is the so-called rooting reflex. It is best seen in a hungry baby or at least one that has not just fed. If something is stroked against a cheek the baby turns towards the object and will mouth it if he makes contact with his lips.

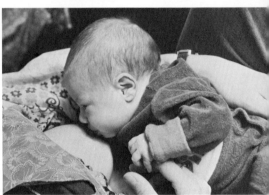

Development of the senses

An infant's powers of visual search are even more impressive.[2] If a bright object is moved slowly through the field of view a baby will move his head and eyes to follow it. If the movement is small the eyes alone move in a series of short jerks (*saccads*) just as in adults. With larger movements the head and eyes move. Not only is the baby able to move his eyes to follow the object as it is perceived to move over the retina, but these movements are coordinated with those of muscles in the neck that control the position of the head. Another sophisticated skill is the ability to locate a sound source in space and turn to look at it. This can be seen if you stand beside a baby just out of the line of sight and speak softly. Usually the baby will turn to look at you. Abilities like this are central to human communication with its emphasis on sight and sound. Another indication of this is the demonstration that newborns are more likely to respond to speech sounds than any other kind of noise. In fact, when psychologists first tried to investigate babies' hearing they used pure tones and other very artificial stimuli and ended up very unimpressed with infants. However, when more natural sounds like speech were used, a dramatic improvement in abilities was found.

The selective attention to speech sounds have great advantages for infants because it leads them into our dominant mode of communication. It is as if they are born with the knowledge that speech is important and that they must listen to what is going on to learn to speak themselves. Without this selective ability an infant would be truly a blank slate and it is hard to see that they would ever learn to speak and understand speech. It would be a monumental task to sort out which sounds are part of human communication and which are irrelevant. A blank slate baby

Selective attention indeed! When I'm on the 'box', everyone is transfixed.

55

would be as likely to sing like the family budgerigar or bark like a dog as utter words in the second year of life.

Selective viewing

The visual system also has constraints at birth which make it more likely that the baby will attend to signals of social relevance. The focus of the eyes is fixed so that objects about 20cm away are most clearly seen and it is not until about four months that full accommodation (focussing) is present as in an adult.[3] 20cm is about the average distance face to face when an adult holds a

Shimmering balls of bubbly delight—But baby still needs to find out where they've gone.

small baby so a newborn is more likely to be looking at faces, rich sources of social signals, than more distant and less socially important objects. Preference tests have demonstrated that young infants will look at faces rather than less socially relevant but equally complex patterns. The concept of a face is an adult construction and there is no reason to think that a young infant uses the same concepts as adults in his perceptions of the world. An accurate but clumsy way of describing an infant's behaviour is that he prefers to look at visual patterns that adult psychologists classify as faces.

In other ways the infant's visual system is much like that of adults. They can see colours (reds and blues seem to be their favourites) and their acuity (sharpness of vision) is only a little less than that of adults.

12 months
Has wide range of co-ordinated vision in all directions. Drops and throws toys forwards, watching them fall to ground, and also in correct direction for those rolling out of sight. Recognises familiar people within range of 20 feet or more and shows great interest in all situations outdoors where movement stimulates interest. Begins to be interested when shown pictures. Has close range vision up to about 10 feet, and will point with index finger at interesting objects or events.

9 months
Very attentive to all visual happenings in immediate surroundings. Will observe and manipulate small objects with much interest. Has good ability at eye and hand co-ordination and observes activities of other people within 10–12 feet for a few moments at a time.

6 months
Has great interest in all surroundings and watches adult activities across room. Will watch objects falling in field of vision. If they roll out of visual field they are 'forgotten' at once. Hand and eye are co-ordinated in grasping close objects. Any squint is now abnormal.

3 months
Shows great interest in human face and will also scan surroundings when held upright. Will follow slowly moving objects held 6–12 inches from face through half-circle. Watches movements of own hands engaging in finger play but cannot co-ordinate hand and eyes.

1 month
Will turn towards light sources and follow gently moving objects held in line of vision at 6–10 inches away. Will watch mother's face during feeding with increasing alertness.

Neonate (a newly born infant)
The neonate has not seen before but adapts quickly, closing eyes against strong light, and turning towards diffuse light sources. Has a limited focal length of approx. 12 inches. Will 'corner' eyes towards sound sources in a reflex manner—vision should thus be tested with a silent object.

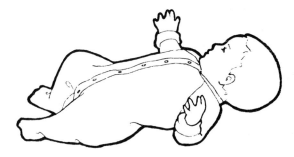

What a child sees

Able to distinguish people

Other senses are equally well developed. Smell has been little investigated but it is easy to show that newborns will turn away from smells that adults find unpleasant. An experiment by an Oxford paediatrician, Aidan Macfarlane, has demonstrated that by ten days a breast-fed baby can distinguish the smell of the breast that has fed him from that of another lactating woman. Macfarlane placed a breast pad on each side of the baby's face and recorded which way he turned. At first the turning was more or less random but after the babies were a week old they increasingly turned towards the breast pad that had been worn by their mother. Similar observations have been made by women who have wet-nursed babies. Though hungry babies will take any breast their behaviour at a strange breast tends to be a little tentative at first, suggesting that they know the difference.

Other research confirms that by ten days of age a baby will respond differently to a new caretaker. Dr. Lou Sander set up an experiment with babies who had been given up by their mothers for adoption.[4] For the first ten days they were looked after by one nurse and then another for the next ten days. Each baby-nurse pair set up their own characteristic style of interaction. So though the two nurses thought that they each behaved similarly with all the babies they looked after, the pattern that emerged was obviously as much a product of the baby's behaviour as the nurse's. But whenever a baby was swapped from one nurse to another, his behaviour went through a sudden change and there was often a good deal of crying. He obviously noticed the change and seemed to resent it. But from this kind of evidence we cannot say that a baby recognises a caretaker at ten days of age, because recognition in the adult sense involves the perception of an individual as a person unlike all others. It is not until later ages that we have evidence of this sort of ability. It would be more accurate to say that babies respond in different ways to different caretakers and seem to prefer the familiar to the novel. At this age they seem to have no difficulties in adapting to several regular caretakers, but there is probably a limit to the number they can become familiar with. It is not known what this number is, but it is surely exceeded in the larger hospital prem nurseries where a baby may well encounter 50 nurses during a stay of a couple of months. With this number of caretakers a baby does not have a chance to learn the patterns of behaviour characteristic to any one caretaker. Familiarity allows the development of expectancies and their confirmation (or otherwise) in future encounters. These are important in developing a knowledge of the social world, particularly that to some extent an individual's behaviour is consistent and that your own behaviour can depend on this.

Preference for sweetness

Newborns can distinguish the broad categories of taste—sweet, sour and salty—and show a preference for sweet things. They will try to expel things that adults find taste unpleasant. The preference for sweetness is not unexpected as human breast milk tastes sweet—much sweeter than cows' milk. But if given substances like sugar solutions which are sweeter than this they still show a preference. This initial preference for sweet things can be developed if babies are given a lot of sugar as it seems to be addictive. Given the damaging effects of refined sugars on health some parents try to avoid giving infants sugar, and it seems it may be possible to reduce children's fondness for sweet things if sugars are avoided in infancy.

Adaptation is the key

Thus infant behaviour can be roughly divided into those patterns which are an adaptation to the special dependent world of infants and those which are precursors of adult behaviour. It is through the adaptation to the world of infancy that adult patterns emerge. The special world of infancy requires special adaptation but it is this very world that leads a baby to adulthood. It is the dependency that places the infant in a position where it can develop the social skills required for adulthood in a cultured species. The ability to develop these skills is the essence of human development, so being able to survive successfully as a human baby in the end comes to the same thing as being able to grow up as a full member of our culture.

Perhaps what is most astonishing about a human baby is that it is able to adapt so well to such varied cultures with their different child-rearing techniques. There is no essential biological difference between a newborn strapped to a cradleboard in a Navajo hogan and one in a cot in a white-tiled, neon-lit nursery in a large American hospital. Throughout the first year social contacts may be brief and almost entirely limited to one person, usually a mother, or may take up most of the day and involve many family members and friends. In either situation, development is surprisingly similar with milestones, like the age at which talking and walking are achieved, being almost the same. This tells us that not only can infants adapt to these very dissimilar social worlds but that from the dissimilarity they are able to construct their own similar environments for development. They actively select from what goes on around them.

This selection, together with their own plasticity, allows similar development from dissimilar environments. It used to be thought that the similarity in development could only be explained if we assumed that much of development was innate; that is to say that it is inbuilt like an alarm clock ready to go off at the appropriate age. What we now understand is a kind of paradox that the regularities in development arise not from preprogrammed inflexibility but a flexibility and plasticity that allows infants to use different environments in very variable ways to achieve the same ends. What is fixed in human infants is this flexible capacity to reach the same ends by very different routes.

5   Life with infants

For many people, the realisation of how different life with children can be from the life of childless (or childfree) adults, comes slowly in the two or three months after delivery. During labour, delivery and the immediate post-partum period, the baby and parents are likely to get a lot of attention and there is a novelty about all that happens. But a few weeks later feelings can change. The novelty has worn off and days are completely filled with feeding and cleaning the baby. Nights are disturbed by crying. Constant childcare seems to stretch ahead into an unlimited future unrelieved by any of the activities that were important to the parents before the baby was born. Parents feel that things may never be the same again and are very panicky about what they have let themselves in for. The baby is, of course, sweet and adorable—at least that is what is easiest to say in public—but privately they may bitterly resent the constant demands for attention and wonder how they could have been misled by all the glossy pictures of smiling, well-polished babies dressed in immaculate clothes.

Reactions, of course, vary, as do capacities to cope and what needs to be coped with. But the point I want to emphasise is that our culture tends to idealise parenthood and many parents find themselves let down with a bump when they discover that reality does not square up with the image.

The harsh realities

It is not hard to see why the Madonna and Child image of motherhood is still so pervasive as it is closely linked to assumptions about the position of women in our society. At root the basic assumption of our society is that a fulfilled life for a woman is marriage and the rearing of children; that while men find satisfaction in the world of work, women will be at home providing physical and emotional comforts for their husbands and their children. Though assumptions of this kind are being continually challenged, not least by women who reject wifehood and motherhood as sufficient in themselves to provide lifelong satisfaction, they are so deeply ingrained that they maintain a misleading view of parenthood.

In the next section of this chapter I want to analyse some of the difficulties that parents commonly face with young children and

Had a late night last night . . .

. . . I suppose I have to face it—life with me is not always easy.'

then to go on to consider some of the ways in which these difficulties can be alleviated or avoided. I will first approach this from a social point of view; looking at the kinds of situations in which parents live and have lived in the past and then move to the level of parents' feelings and experiences.

Those were the days

In many discussions of present-day family life people hark back to earlier times when, they argue, family life was happier and more satisfying than today. They are apt to contrast the typical nuclear family of today with its isolated parents and children with earlier times when, they say, families were extended (three generations and possibly other kin in the household or nearby) and much more integrated into the community. The extended family, or so the argument goes, provided parents with more support than they generally receive today and gave a much richer and more varied life for children. When things go wrong, we may often try to recreate some Utopian past, a golden age when the sun always shone, unlike the drab days of the present. But the good old days may be as much a product of our selective memory and romantic fantasies as any historical reality.

In recent years historians have been paying increasing attention to the history of family life.[1] Though their research is far from complete, it is worth discussing some of what we know about our recent past because it gives us a valuable perspective from which to look at the present. An examination of the historical record will also dispel any notion of a golden age that has passed. Perhaps this is no bad thing because it should make us more realistic about any present difficulties and in turn should lead to more effective remedies. As today, families in the past were very varied, between places, at different times and for the members of the various social groups of any society. An English sixteenth-century peasant family led a life quite unlike the aristocrats of the time and each of these may have differed quite considerably from their equivalents in say France or Italy. But to make the contrasts with the present, I will discuss two rather generalised examples from England: a family in a village in the sixteenth century and an urban middle-class family in the nineteenth century.

More people, less privacy

The first thing we may notice about our family from the earlier period is that the household is larger than an average one of the present day, perhaps six or seven members rather than three or four, but the larger size is not made up by the inclusion of three generations. Instead, the household might have consisted of a man and his wife, their three or four children and one or two other people who are unrelated and who act as household servants. The age of marriage was late, usually 27 or 28 and because the life-span was somewhat shorter than today the chances of grandparents still being alive much beyond the time when their first grandchildren were born was small. Servants, however, were very common and perhaps a half or more of all households contained them. These servants left their own homes when they were quite small children, often between seven and ten years old, and might remain in their new homes until they married or perhaps returned to their original family home at the death of their parents to take over the farm. They lived as members of their 'adoptive' families, sharing meals and work with all the other members of the household. Another thing that would strike us about the household would be the lack of privacy. Parents, children and servants would not only often share the same room to sleep in but sharing beds was also common. This was not simply a matter of poverty and lack of living space, but that the same value was not given to an individual's private and personal space as it is today.

Of course, it is much easier for historians to establish matters such as the number of people who lived in a house and the age of marriage (available via church records) than to obtain an accurate picture of fine details of people's daily life and their feelings. On these issues our information is sketchy and must be partly guesswork.

Marriage was probably an economic arrangement in which each partner provided some of the work required for the household's survival. Not infrequently marriages were arranged by parents. In general men were more likely to work outside on the land, while women worked in the house. But as all work went on in and around the home, there was probably a good deal of give and take in who did what. Roles would not have been as segregated as in more recent times. Indoor, as well as outdoor, tasks produced goods required for home consumption and for sale or exchange. Production of cloth and beer, for instance, was often carried out in homes and was largely seen as women's work. Given the important direct economic place of many of the jobs largely done by women, it has been suggested that marriage was more of an equal partnership than it became later when many women were confined to housework and childcare.

Birth control

Infant mortality was high with perhaps one-third of all children dying before they reached adolescence. But this alone was not the only reason why couples did not have larger families. Some kind of birth control seems to have been used. Some historians have suggested that the usual 18 months period of lactation with its partial suppression of ovulation would be sufficient to account for the usual spacings between births while others believe that specific contraceptive techniques must have been employed. Babies were usually swaddled for the first six months or so.

We do not really know how exclusively childcare would fall to the mother, but given that there was a good deal of sharing of domestic work it seems unlikely that this would not also apply to childcare. Anyway given the close physical proximity of all the household members it seems likely that the person nearest to the child would provide the necessary attention. If this was so, infants formed more close relations than is usual today and would become attached to all the household members. Overall, discipline seems to have been strict and the hitting of young children was common. Some of this can be accounted for by a need for control in the confined living space. But control of bodily functions and prudery were largely absent: indeed with children living in such close proximity with adults it is difficult to see how children could have been prevented from having a full knowledge of all human activities from the earliest years. Toilet training does not seem to have been an issue for parents and was as lax as all standards of hygiene. Similarly expressions of infantile sexuality seem to have been accepted as normal and not frowned on.

Differing attitudes

Some writers have seen this world as one in which childhood was a nightmare. Certainly it was no golden age but if we use our own standards inappropriately we may distort the picture. Swaddling (called an 'infant prison' by some later writers) and the sending out of young children as servants have been used as evidence of the punitive attitude to children. However, there is nothing particularly cruel and punitive about the way swaddling is used in some cultures today, so we should not assume that things were different in the past. Seeing swaddling in this way says more about our attitudes to babies than the quality of life for children in this period. In the same way it is easy to misinterpret the early departure of children from the parents' house. Some psychiatrists would argue that such practices would give rise to life-long psychological problems. However, in several cultures today (West Africa, for instance) similar practices still exist and investigations have not revealed any later psychological problems that seem to be associated with it. Indeed, in some sections of our own society it is the practice to send five- or six-year-olds away to boarding school, which in several ways seems more damaging than transplantation to another household—a point confirmed by some contemporary autobiographies.

Clearly in this pre-industrial world children were seen in a very different way from today. For a start, childhood was a much shorter period than today as by the age of six or seven children were expected to work. Formal education was more or less non-existent and children learned about work by watching others and working alongside them. In one important sense, parents probably had an easier time of it than today because infancy and childhood were not seen as being an important formative period. What parents did with their children was not seen to have a crucial effect on adult character and personality. The only version of this at all common was the doctrine of original sin which meant that parents had the responsibility of knocking (literally) a child's innate wickedness out of him. But the doctrine was not universal and at many levels development was seen simply as inevitable. Special efforts to influence children were a waste of time as they would grow up in the image of their parents.

Patriarchal society

The atmosphere in a nineteenth-century middle-class home

stands in stark contrast to both the pre-industrial household and a present-day family. The family of the early Victorian entrepreneur, the kind of family which owed its existence to the profits made from the growing industries or the bureaucratic occupations that industrialisation spawned, represents a high point in patriarchy and the repression of the expression of feeling. Family development over the last century can be seen as a slow liberalisation from these values.

Households were large—seven or eight children, three-quarters of whom were likely to survive to adulthood and as many servants as the husband felt were necessary to demonstrate the social status and prestige of the household. Now there was a maximum of role segregation between the husband and wife. He went out to work and his own male-dominated social world while his wife remained at home, entertained her female friends and graced the household with her feminine presence. The values of privacy, decorum and duty pervaded everything. The wider family was much less central than in the pre-industrial world. The often cooperative give and take between family members and neighbours was replaced by more distant competitive relations in which social standing dominated all aspects of life. This made the household a much more inward-looking and isolated place.

Traditional parental roles are no longer so clearly defined. Dad does some mothering to share the burden—and joy—of a double load.

Segregation and status

Within the home status differences were everything. Wives deferred to husbands, servants to masters and mistresses, children to parents and kitchen maids to parlour maids. Home was

designed to provide privacy for everyone and as much segregation of the sexes as possible. It was unthinkable that a servant could eat at the same table as his or her employer.

Children were segregated from adults. The nursery was created as a special space where the servants would look after them. Contact between children and their parents was very limited and all day-to-day caretaking was carried out by servants. Breast-feeding had declined and was frequently replaced by wet-nursing or bottle feeding. At a very young age many boys and a few girls were sent away to boarding school. Psychologically too, parents were far from their children. Expression of emotion and feeling was severely reduced. Men were not expected to show any feeling in public (this is the age of the stiff upper lip) while women absented themselves from emotional situations by fainting.

Though fainting may have been encouraged by tight corsets and meagre diets, it was a basic part of the whole psychological role women were brought up to play. They were taught to feel weak and feeble and were as far as possible sheltered from any mention of sexuality and the functions of elimination. As Dr. William Acton was able to assert in his famous statement, 'The majority of women (happily for them) are not very much troubled with sexual feelings of any kind'. As far as marriage was concerned, he went on to say: 'She submits to her husband, but only to please him, and but for the desire for maternity, would far rather be relieved of his attentions.' Of course, many men sought outlets away from the repressive atmosphere of their homes and the other side of this Victorian life was prostitution,

Contemporary candour—a matter-of-factness about the body that is a far cry from Victorian prudery.

which often was the only form of employment available to women among the urban poor.

Manners maketh the man

From the earliest age great attention was paid to a child's toilet training and such matters as table manners. Any hint of the expression of sexuality in children was punished. Some doctors went to the extreme of advocating placing children in strait-jackets to prevent masturbation.

Victorian middle-class parents did believe that they could influence the development of their children but their concerns were for their children to take their rightful place in the world. This was to be done by rigid disciplining and the inculcation of required values and appropriate formal education. The achievement was seen as a struggle in which duty and honour would triumph over sensuality and feeling. Things did you good if they hurt. Though a good deal of attention was paid to children it was not a period that could be described as child-centred, as the emotional needs of children were not considered to be important. Though games and play did form a part of nursery life, most of what went on was very much geared to the requirements of adult life.

On the other side of the coin

The life I have described above was, of course, very different from the experience of the working class who were moving to the towns in increasing numbers in the search for work. Like their rural forebears they accepted child labour or at least were driven to it because their meagre wages were needed for the survival of the household. But now such labour was not done in the household or on the land alongside other household members but was transferred to the factory or mine.

Families were large but mortality was very high in the city slums, higher probably than in many rural pre-industrial communities. Less breast-feeding and early marriage were part of the reason for the greater number of pregnancies. Often families could not cope with all the children that were born and infanticide was widespread. Parents might smother their children or hand them over to foster parents in situations where death was almost certain. Under such conditions there was not much scope for the prudency that characterised the rising middle classes. However, towards the end of the nineteenth century when living standards and housing began to improve a bit, such values did begin to percolate down the social scale. Indeed as this movement occurred, the slow liberalisation of childhood and decline in patriarchy began to influence the middle classes.

After this glimpse at our history, I want to return to the consideration of the social situation of present day families. Here, as when considering the past, we must be conscious of the dangers of over-generalisation. In the main my remarks will concern English middle- and lower middle-class families and will apply with varying accuracy to other social groups and other parts of the industrialised world.

The average family

What are the key features of our families?[2] We tend to marry fairly young, in our early twenties, and have an average of two children fairly soon after marriage. Our households are small, usually only containing parents and children. Links with the wider network of relatives are not particularly strong and on the

'Ships Ahoy'—real or toy, keeping the flow of fun at a high ebb.

whole the family is fairly isolated. Social life usually centres on the family and couples spend the bulk of their leisure time together and with their children. Work and home life are very separate. Work (in the sense of waged work) is almost always something done outside the household in another place. There are very few remnants of the blurred line between household work and earning work that was typical of the pre-industrial household.

The roles of wife and husband are separate but less so than for the Victorian middle-class family. Women do not often give up paid work on marriage and a majority continue working throughout marriage with only relatively brief periods when they spend all their time within the home. Because of the smaller number of children and the longer lifespan a much briefer proportion of a woman's life is spent in childcare than has been true in the past. Within the home women continue to be responsible for the bulk of childcare and domestic work. Usually this is still the case when both wife and husband have jobs outside the home and in many countries is institutionally reflected in things like maternity leave. This is now fairly generally available, while paternity leave is much rarer. In recent decades there have been some shifts in the distribution of work within the home but it is still only a small minority of men who share responsibility for their children and take an equal part in their care.

Life after Freud and Spock

Our society is often described as child-centred. Certainly, we pay a lot of attention to the needs of children. But perhaps the main thing that sets us apart from earlier times is that we have a very strong belief that what we do with children and, indeed, young babies, matters for their future development. There is not a great deal of agreement about what kinds of early experience lead to particular aspects of later development but there is a general consensus that early experience matters.[3] Our approach to childcare is less punitive than that of some of our forebears and

Attention and affection to demonstrate love—and perhaps also to foster his emotional growth.

distraction and reward are now seen to be important techniques in teaching discipline. Though few English parents would agree with the old saying 'A child, a wife and a walnut tree, the more they are beaten, the better they be', most, in fact, do hit their children before their first birthday and some use physical punishment daily. The belief that children should not be spoilt is our modern version of the older belief that original sin must be knocked out of children and it is still widespread. Beyond this belief is the need to control and discipline children. In the modern period we have been much more preoccupied with their education and their emotional growth.

As universal education grew up in the nineteenth century it

69

was quite common for two- and three-year-olds to be sent to school. This was probably less because their parents thought that formal education should begin at this age, than that the schools provided a convenient child-minding service. By the beginning of this century school entry (in England) had been restricted to five-year-olds. However, over the last fifty years there has been a growing movement to provide education for the under-fives. An early example was the Montessori nursery school movement. Today many proponents of nursery schools see them as providing formal education for children as well as the more traditional role of a place where children can play and can be looked after safely. Infancy has been influenced in the same way. Certain parental activities have been encouraged because they are thought to have important cognitive (educational) advantages for children. Speaking to children in ways thought to expand their knowledge of language and providing 'educational' toys are two examples. Another is a recent book which has been popular among parents called *How to teach your baby how to read*.

Long-term effects

'Rub a dub dub ... thanks for the grub ... yeah yeah yeah!' Emotional rituals of this kind are important for both baby and parent.

At every point in history it seems likely that some parents have been concerned with the emotional happiness and well-being of their children. Perhaps such concerns are more widespread today: it is hard to know. But like the interest in early education there is now an interest in long-term consequences. A satisfying emotional life is thought to be important for a child because it has beneficial effects for adulthood. An example of this is the

campaign to open children's wards in hospitals to free visiting by parents. It is obvious to anyone who has visited a traditional children's ward that many children are distressed and upset by an admission to hospital. However, this never seemed a sufficient reason to allow parents free contact with their children or to let them stay overnight in the hospital. But when it was suggested that the separation from parents resulting from a hospital stay might have adverse effects on *adult* personality and social functioning, those responsible for the hospital care of children began to change their policies.

So it is not a concern with the here-and-now that is seen as most important but possible long-term consequences. Such a belief causes much anxiety for parents because they are seen as the people who have the responsibility of ensuring that children grow up in the right emotional climate. Their task is made harder because there is not a clear agreement about what the right climate is. So whatever they do there is the possibility that a child will not develop satisfactorily and they are the people who are likely to be blamed.

Despite the fact that this journey does not seem to be getting anywhere, frequent family outings provide a vehicle for the child's drive towards emotional security.

The idea that the quality of a child's relationship with his parents has long-term effects was popularised by the writings of Sigmund Freud at the end of the last century.[4] His ideas at first met with great resistance, not least because he described children's sexuality and gave it great prominence in his theories. But gradually, as there was a retreat from Victorian prudery, his ideas became more widely accepted, especially in the United States. A central concept in Freud's system is repression—the notion that a painful experience or feeling would apparently be forgotten but in fact is stored in the unconscious to resurface in

some indirect form later in life. Many of the events that Freud thought were responsible for neurotic behaviour in adulthood occurred in early childhood in the relationship with parents. He suggested that the success or failure of these early relations was closely connected to an adult's ability to form and maintain satisfactory heterosexual relationships in adulthood. By the 1920s and 1930s some of Freud's ideas were being translated into advice for parents. For instance, Freudians warned parents against early and sudden weaning and an overconcern with toilet training, as they felt these were often at the root of neurotic problems.

For the purpose of charting changing attitudes to childcare it is not important to establish whether or not Freud's account of psychological development is accurate. The important point is that by the 1940s the idea that relationships with parents in some way form a prototype for adult relationships and that the quality of the former would be reflected in the latter had become very widespread. It is this, together with the social isolation of the nuclear family, that gives present-day parenthood its unique qualities.

'The child is father to the man,' they say— but how much of an impact do early experiences really have on their future lives?

Divorce and remarriage

It is commonly said that the current high rates of divorce represent the end of the family and it is implied that this is a very new phenomenon. Certainly the statistics are startling: a projection of present divorce rates indicates that only half of all American children born today can expect to reach adulthood having their two parents still married to one another. The proportion for English children is two-thirds. However, the statistics do not show any decline in the popularity of marriage.

A fairytale marriage that may well become yet another statistic in today's soaring divorce rate.

Rates of remarriage are very high and a greater percentage of the whole population marries than in any previous period for which we have records. Despite this increasing tendency to change marital partners it may also be true that today children can expect a longer unbroken relationship with their parents than at previous times. In the past, the later age at marriage and the higher adult death rate meant that many more parents died before their children grew up. In addition, we do not often send our children away from home before adolescence. Our relationships with our children tend to be long and close and more often than not persist until marriage. Difficulties over housing mean that in England many couples begin their married life in the home of one of their parents.

The isolation of the new mother

Some of the common problems that parents face in living with infants stem from the isolation that many women experience when they are at home with a small baby.[5] This isolation not only arises from the structure of the small nuclear family with its weakened links with the more distant kin, but also because of the common expectations of mutual dependence of the couple. Before their children arrive a lot of their social life consists of activities undertaken together not necessarily involving any other friends and family members. For many women, the social contacts at work form an important part of their social world. This and much of what she did with her husband disappears once she has children and she is left at home all day, physically and socially isolated. Before she had children she may not have spent much time in the neighbourhood of the home so may not have many friends in the range that can be covered easily with a young baby. The table below shows who English mothers called on for help in the period immediately after their babies were born.[6] It demonstrates how only the close family are significantly involved (and only female relatives) and how friends and neighbours become more important as more children are born. This is presumably because as they live in a neighbourhood longer they make more local friends.

Sources of mothers' help	Number of children			All mothers
	1 (%)	2 (%)	3 (%)	
Husband	89	90	87	89
Mother	50	52	45	49
Mother-in-law	27	25	25	25
Sister or sister-in-law	26	27	30	27
Other relatives	11	9	13	12
Friends or neighbours	25	38	48	35
Local authority home help	—	1	—	1
Paid help	—	2	2	2
Other	5	4	3	4
No-one	3	2	2	2

What stems from this isolation? One of the commonest results is depression. Surveys in Britain have shown that up to 40 per cent of women with children under five-years-old suffer from depression serious enough to warrant psychiatric treatment. The link with social isolation is demonstrated by the fact that rates are much lower for married women of the same age group who do not have children, and for women with children who go out to work. Pointing in the same direction is the finding that women who have a close confiding relationship with their husband, a relative or friend are less likely to suffer depression.[7] Studies of this problem point to the existence of an enormous amount of misery and unhappiness. It has implications beyond the women concerned. Children of depressed mothers can suffer and it often causes problems in the marriage relationship. This is one reason why nine to twelve months after a child is born is a very common time for a marriage to break up.

Link between depression and parental divorce
Of course not all isolated women with young children suffer from depression. Interestingly enough the chance of developing depression is also related to the mother's own childhood. Separation from her own mother before she was eleven significantly increases vulnerability to depression. We now have a whole series of studies that confirm a link between childhood experience and features of adult life connected with parenthood. Specifically loss of either parent in childhood is connected to higher rates of depression, problems in child-rearing and problems for the infant. But it appears to be crucial how the

separation has come about. Loss through parental death does not seem to be important—it is when it occurs after marital separation or divorce that the problems are likely to arise.[8] Divorce often means that children lose contact with one parent (most often the father) though this is often avoidable. Retaining links with both parents can be vital.

The reasons why parental divorce and separation can have damaging effects on children are threefold. First divorce often means the creation of a single-parent family. On average, these are both economically and socially poorer than two-parent families. Two parents can be more available for children than one and are able to provide a more varied social world. Lack of money has many direct and indirect effects on children and is connected with things like poor progress at school. A second effect of divorce on children arises through the quarrelling and disorganisation that usually precede the actual separation.

When adults are caught in emotional tangles they have little time or energy for children. The final and perhaps most important reason of all is that children usually feel considerable anger and loss of the parent who leaves the home. The departing spouse is not only leaving a wife or husband but he or she is also abandoning the children. Lack of contact after a divorce reinforces the feeling and children often feel that they have done something to drive the parent away. This can make them feel very guilty and unworthy and they may grow up with a continuing low self-evaluation. Feelings of worthlessness are often characteristic of people who suffer from depression.

This link between parental separation and the development of children can be seen as a partial validation of the broad Freudian belief in the importance of childhood. However, we must also note that studies which have sought long-term consequences of less traumatic childhood events than separation have failed to demonstrate links. Punitive toilet training and early weaning, for instance, do not seem to have predictable effects. This is perhaps testimony to the infant's great powers of adaptation and recuperation. Specific experiences of this kind may well have effects on infants, but they do not have an influence that can be picked up years later, because the effect is lost among all the changes and chances of a human life. But we should not take the failure to demonstrate long-term effects as a reason to wean children early. We need to think more of the immediate consequences of such actions on infants and seek ways of rearing our children and living our own lives without causing unnecessary stress to each other.

Mother–infant relationship

A consequence of the frequent isolation of women at home with children is that the relationship between mother and infant becomes all-important and dominates all the others that infants may have. This emphasis on the mother–infant relationship is probably a relatively new phenomenom in the history of the family. Some psychologists have taken it for granted and seen it

Mother and baby—a classic relationship that has long enjoyed romantic exclusivity . . .

. . . but current research shows that closeness with more than one adult figure is important.

as the necessary and sufficient basis for the development of children. John Bowlby, for example, has argued that an unbroken relationship with a mother or permanent mother-figure is essential for adult health. As we have seen already the evidence obtained by comparing a situation where a mother has died with a separation following divorce does not support this view. Furthermore where a child has an unbroken relationship with a mother but has lost a father, separation effects are seen showing that it is misleading to put all the emphasis on the relationship with the mother.

Current evidence supports the view that children are most likely to develop satisfactorily if they grow up with several strong and close relationships and that there are disadvantages in spending a high proportion of time with a single person. Not only do different relationships have different things to offer an infant, but moving from one known person to another is in itself a valuable learning experience for them. An exclusive relationship with one parent can create a situation like that of a fish in an aquarium. Because the fish is constantly surrounded by water it has no opportunity to learn what the properties of water are. If an infant is constantly with one person he may learn little about relationships and find it more difficult to get a knowledge of his own identity separate from other people. It has been suggested that because many children grow up in our culture in the more or less exclusive care of their mothers there is tendency to produce very dependent adults who seek to form suffocatingly close and exclusive adult relationships mirroring their childhood experience. These in turn may perpetuate for another generation the isolated nuclear family situation so the cycle goes on for another generation.

The idea that mothers should have sole charge of their young children certainly contributes to the problems of depression and isolation. Few adults find the exclusive company of infants a very satisfactory social life. But fear of damaging infants by leaving them with other people can deter mothers from seeking adult company. However, as I have pointed out, giving infants the opportunity to form relationships with other adults (and children) far from being damaging has a very positive aspect.

In broad terms it is easy to state the conditions that would relieve many of the common problems experienced by the parents of infants. The care of an infant needs to be shared between the parents and between them and other adults. Parents need their own social life and time away from the demands of young children. We need to be less anxious and concerned about creating long-term psychological problems for our children and put more emphasis on providing a satisfactory life for all family members in the present. The persisting belief that men are unwilling or unable to care for young children needs to be constantly challenged. But having stated the broad conditions it is another matter to put them into practice in individual cases. Demands of employment may impose heavy constraints as do many social conventions and beliefs. Parents may often need to have a strong faith in themselves and in what they want to do to create a satisfactory life. In this chapter I have been particularly concerned to point out that erroneous beliefs about infants—especially the supposed need for a mother to be constant and exclusive caretaker—have often prevented the evolution of family life in desirable directions.

Sibling rivalry

Throughout most of this book, I have talked as if all babies were alone with their parents. But, of course, the majority have older brothers and sisters. Parents are usually concerned about the possibility of jealousy and rivalry. Siblings, particularly if they are well into the toddler stage or older, are usually very interested in the changes in their mother through pregnancy and the new baby. The first reaction to a newborn, much like that of adults, is to want to touch and hold him. But often these first reactions may be followed by signs of resentment and anger. A toilet-trained toddler may revert to bed wetting or demand again an apparently forgotten bottle.

The strength of these reactions seem to depend on the kinds of relationships that existed with the parents and others before the new baby's birth and the extent to which old established patterns are disturbed. If the older child is used to spending most of his time with his mother and their relationship has an exclusive quality, he will be deposed by the new baby and is likely to resent it. But if he has several strong relationships and can find attention from others when one or other of his parents is tied up with the baby things are likely to be much easier for him. He is bound to want to do things with the baby and prohibitions are likely to increase any sense of inclusion he may have. Just as a baby changes the lives of parents, it changes the life of the siblings too,

Does she greet her new sister with hostility or with welcoming affection? It often depends on parent-child relationships before baby's birth.

but a toddler's resources for coping are more limited and they will need more help and support to make an easy adjustment. In the working out of new routines space needs to be found for older siblings so that they get some periods at least where they can still feel that they are at the centre of the stage. This, of course, adds to the pressures on parents in the first few months but in the long run awareness of the siblings' needs at this stage can do much to prevent a little rivalry becoming a deeper resentment.

Child abuse

One consequence of the way that motherhood is idealised in our society is that it makes it very difficult for parents to express any negative feelings they may have about their children, especially when they are very young. The conventional view is that motherhood and fatherhood, each in their rather different ways, are totally fulfilling for adults. Motherhood is represented as the culmination of a woman's life and as such it is expected that a woman will show nothing but love for her baby, the object of her fulfilment. It is hard to imagine the Madonna being angry with the Child. But all close human relationships have positive and negative elements, and those with infants are no exception. At least occasional frustration, irritation and anger are universal. The problem is often that because the existence or expression of such feelings is not socially sanctioned, parents can become very guilty when they feel such things. This guilt can contribute to feelings of inadequacy as a parent and a poor self-image

The discussion of child abuse illustrates the damaging effects that the Madonna and Child idealisation can have. Parents who injure their children are sometimes depicted as monsters whose feelings are quite outside any normal range. A few do suffer from serious mental illness but most do not. They are simply parents who are under more stress than most and are unable to control their angry feelings about their children and express them in a violent form. I do not wish to condone the violent treatment of children but in dealing with the problem it is essential to recognise the stresses under which many parents live and understand the ways in which stress exacerbates negative feelings towards children. Successful prevention of child abuse consists of trying to reduce the stresses and in increasing the parents' own controls so that angry feelings are not acted out in physical attacks.

Like father, like son
Studies of child abuse show that it is often the extreme case of the general situations that I have considered in this chapter.[9] It is more common in socially isolated families and where the child's behaviour is especially difficult and frustrating. Victims are often handicapped children. It is more likely to occur when parents get on badly and do not have a close confiding relationship and do

not cooperate over sharing childcare. Where parents themselves have been treated in a violent or abusive way as children they are more likely to treat their own children in the same way. This is probably because the kinds of deprivation that create stresses for parents and lead to an increased chance of violence towards children tend to be inherited by each new generation. Another reason is that a child who receives violence from his parents is less likely to develop the controls over his own acting out which are needed to prevent violence.

Parents who feel angry with young children should talk about their feelings with their co-parent or anyone else who they trust. They should try and work out what the situations are that make them angry and see if there are ways in which they can be avoided. Feeding is often a centre for anger. Infants may seem to make a mess deliberately or take their food especially slowly when the parent is in a rush. A series of confrontations over feeding can turn it into a continuing battleground. There are several ways in which the heat can be taken out of these situations. If the problem is that the child is throwing food onto the floor, it is perhaps possible to remove the food more promptly when the baby seems to have taken what he wants. Or it is possible to try to give the child what he seems to like rather than what the parents may think he ought to have. Children thrive on the most unlikely diets and seem good at selecting the things that suit them best even though this may not conform to what is laid down in the childcare manuals.

The real root of the problem
Often if parents find that they are becoming very irritated with their children it is because there is some other problem in their lives which is worrying them. Especially where a parent is alone with a baby for long periods of time, it is not very surprising that the baby becomes the butt of their frustrations. Here the need is to identify the true problem and see what can be done about it. Very often some improvement in the living situation will do wonders for the parent–child relationship.

It is often claimed that rates of child abuse are increasing and have never been higher. Precise statistics are impossible to obtain for something that occurs within the privacy of the home. However, it seems most unlikely that current figures are higher than a century ago. Physical punishment of children was much more common then and they were generally treated in a more punitive and controlled way. This must frequently have spilled over into very serious abuse. The large families and poor housing, especially in the urban slums, led to intolerable stresses on parents and from what records we have we know that infanticide, neglect and abandonment were common. Today material conditions have improved immensely, but this has not entirely done away with the problem. The isolated nuclear family is sometimes an explosive mixture of bottled-up emotion and child abuse can happen among those with the highest standards of living.

*Fun, rivalry and an
inevitable victor—
all the ingredients of
a structured game
without the need for
language.*

6 Communication and games

If you stop to think about a conversation or indeed any kind of social interaction between adults you will soon realise what a complicated sequence of events is involved. A conversation depends on a series of unspoken agreements between the two participants. Normally each will be speaking the same language. This implies that a whole set of assumptions about the meanings of words will be shared. But there are other less obvious assumptions about the content of what is said; that what each says will in some way relate to what the other has said or, if there is a sudden change in subject, that the speaker will signal this. Another is that the speakers will signal the beginning or end of a conversation in some special way. Occasionally a participant may break off in the middle of a conversation and move away but this carries its own social meaning.

Conversations have a structure in time: one person talks while the other listens. If one person breaks into what the other is saying, again, this carries a special social meaning.

But listening to the words of a conversation does not tell us all of what goes on. Much is conveyed by non verbal signals—smiles, looks of surprise, the body position of the speaker and so on. In addition, information is carried by the tone of the voice, pauses in speech and many other subtle cues.

Silent language

The basis of human communication, whether or not it involves speech, is a series of social conventions, rules by which we can interpret and understand all the signals and cues.[1] During the long period of dependency that characterises human childhood a child grows into his culture by assimilating its particular conventions of social life. During infancy, by definition, an infant does not speak but nevertheless by the end of the first year he has developed considerable knowledge of the social conventions of his immediate world. Without speaking he can communicate many of his needs and intentions quite clearly and can play his part in games and other quite complicated social interchanges.

81

A cry that says 'Get me out of this jam—and if I'm ignored any longer I'll just scream and scream and scream . . .'

Getting the right responses

An infant discovers his social world by the responses he receives to his actions. These tell him what his actions mean to those around him and allow him to modify these to produce required responses. During infancy this is not a conscious process, the baby is not working out plans of how to get what he wants but the end product is much what you might expect if he was. Indeed, parents frequently imply or say that their baby has conscious intentions, 'he only does it because he knows it annoys me'. By attributing such intentions to small babies parents create a kind of dialogue or relationship in which the baby is gradually able to develop a sense of his own conscious choice and intention.[2]

But to return to the basic response and reply system. The baby does something and in some unconscious way registers what happens in reply.[3] Even this apparently simple link is quite complex and is rich in learning opportunities as a simple example will show. A baby cries, what happens? The cry may produce no response because the caretaker decides that the baby cannot be hungry and the tone of the cry does not imply that there is anything seriously wrong. A study undertaken in Cambridge found that if baby cried when in his cot the most likely response from the parents was to pick him up and feed him. But the chance of being picked up depended on the time since the last feed. Babies were most likely to be picked up very soon after they have been fed or three-and-a-half to four hours later. Soon after a feed a baby is likely to be picked up because the parent may think he is still hungry or has wind. Three-and-a-half to four hours later corresponds to the usual interval between feeds in the community studied. The chances of a parental response to crying also varied with the time of day—it is much higher during daylight hours than at night. So even this simple example shows how much a baby can potentially learn about his social world from the way in which his cry is or is not responded to. Part of what he learns is not only that caretakers interpret his signals in particular ways (crying is usually seen as an indication of hunger) but that it matters when you do things—day and night are not the same and nor are times before and after feeds and the intervals between.

Crucial timing

Timing is, in fact, a vital characteristic of all social communication. What you do has to be phased in time with the actions of the person you are communicating with. Right from delivery an infant's behaviour has a rhythmical structure and the caretaker's actions are built around this so providing the first beginnings of mutual timing structure seen in all social encounters. Sucking provides an example of this first primitive co-ordination.[4] When a baby sucks it does not do so continuously but in a series of bursts separated by pauses giving it a rhythmical structure. If sucking is recorded with a pressure measuring device you get a record of the kind shown below. When a breast-feeding mother's behaviour is observed it is found that it is fitted around this sucking rhythm. So, for instance, a mother is much more likely to talk to a baby in the pauses between the bursts of sucking than while the baby is actually sucking. So in these very early interactions we can already find the basic rhythmical and reciprocal timing structure of social communication. They provide the infant with an opportunity of learning the first rules of communication. Interestingly enough, observations of bottle feeding show that there is much less co-ordination of mother's talking with the baby's sucking than in breast-feeding. This is probably because bottle feeding is less of an interactive social event than breast-feeding and mutual social interchange occurs at other times in the infant's day.

Playing games

From these first co-ordinated activities social interaction develops quickly and becomes much more complicated. Around six or eight weeks infants begin to smile more frequently and their smiling becomes much easier to elicit predictably. Or in other terms, the baby is able to build it into more complicated social exchanges. A typical game that adults play with infants of this age is to sit opposite them face to face and get them to smile and laugh. This is done by moving the head towards and away from the baby. The baby looks intently at each approach and eventually smiles. Then the baby often turns away from the adult for a little time before turning back to signal his readiness to begin a new sequence.

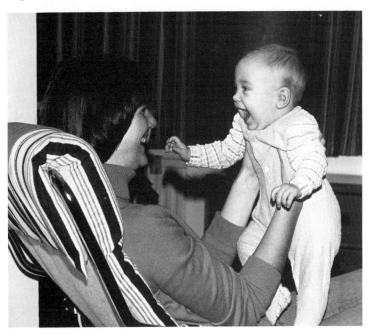

*The trading of smiles—
a form of exchange as
old as mankind.*

Who's doing what first? Imitation is one of easiest and most reward-ing games to play: immediate responses are the best reward for parent and infant alike.

It is easy to show that the infant's role in these games is not passive and that he has an expectation of what the adult is going to do next.[5] This can be done by the adult changing the sequence in some way—breaking the sequence of the approaches for example. Often if this is done the infant breaks off the game by turning away from the adult. After a few months of age, in situations like this babies show a clear sense of surprise. Indeed, this is a common component of the games that parents play. Peek-a-boo and its many variants where people appear and disappear are popular with most infants. In developing these social games, an infant needs both familiarity with their partner so that they can build up a picture for themselves of what is likely to happen and an element of novelty and surprise which enables them to move on to more complex and varied sequences. Parents change their games as an infant grows up providing this variability. A number of familiar partners provide the best conditions for optimal development because each is likely to play rather different games so increasing the variety available to the infant. But their familiarity provides the predictability needed by the infant.

Learning the rules

We can divide the things that infants learn in their social encounters into two categories. First there are the rules and conventions that are known to all members of the culture.[6] These include the meaning of gestures like waving, the expression of emotion, the ways in which we classify things that we can talk about and ultimately the meaning of words. In fact, all the social knowledge we need to have a meaningful conversation with a complete stranger or to behave appropriately in varied social situations. Secondly, there are all the private and particular shared meanings and rituals of behaviour that go on between two people who know each other well. At first the infant is almost restricted to familiar relationships and learning individual idiosyncrasies. But by moving between several familiar relation-ships and by encountering strangers the common features begin to emerge and so knowledge of the culture begins to be built up. For cultural learning a variety of social relationships are required. This is one of the reasons why overexclusive mother–infant relations impede developments.

Fear of strangers

By the middle of the first year surprising events can sometimes frighten babies and produce crying. The so-called fear of strangers which, if it is seen at all, is generally seen around eight or nine months of age is probably a surprise–fear reaction. In babies that are used to seeing a lot of different adults what may be seen is a suddenly and apparently unexplainable surprise–fear reaction to an adult who has not been seen before. A possible explanation of these reactions is that the stranger appears to the baby as similar to someone well known, but the difference from the familiar person is inexplicable to the child and so frightening.

Infrequent reactions of this kind seem to have a different basis

The rough and tumble of play with dad will help his young body grow lithe and strong.

to a general avoidance of new people which is especially frequent if the people are encountered on familiar territory, as in the home. This is a form of shyness. The extent of the reaction seems to depend on how many people a baby has seen before. Where the baby has got to know many adults they are often fairly confident with strangers and will approach them after a short period of hesitation. However, if their previous social experience is of few adults, shyness is often very marked and prolonged.

Physical games

Earlier I described how rhythmical movement like rocking was soothing for most babies. More vigorous movement is often exciting and forms the basis of several games. In some cultures, for instance in the West Indies, such games have become ritualised into a regular daily procedure. The baby is washed and then massaged with a vegetable oil. As his body is rubbed, all the joints are bent and stretched. Then the baby is swung from his arms and upside down from his legs. Finally the baby is tossed in the air and caught several times. Babies who are used to this kind of treatment seem to thoroughly enjoy it and each swing and throw in the air is often accompanied by laughter. Some English parents adopt similar routines and it certainly seems to make their infants' bodies supple and strong. Studies in America and Europe have shown that fathers are more likely to play physical games with their infants while mothers seem to prefer talking and smiling games.

From a very early age, infants behave differently when playing with people and things. I first noticed this in some experiments I was carrying out with eight-week-old babies with Edinburgh psychologist, Colwyn Trevarthen. We were interested in the ways in which babies tracked moving objects with head and eye movements. We had babies sitting in an infant seat beside a table and were rolling very large shiny ball-bearings across the table. These proved to be good objects to elicit tracking as they are very attractive to babies. While tracking, babies would peer intently at the ball-bearing and quite frequently make primitive attempts at reaching. In order to control the speed of roll of the ball-bearing we decided it might be a good idea to automate our apparatus. We thought that we might be able to move the ball-bearing at a constant speed by having a moveable magnet mounted on an arm under the table. But we found that when we tried to move the ball-bearing with a magnet instead of it rolling smoothly it jerked across the table in a very irregular way. The interesting thing was that when this happened the babies behaviour changed completely.

Instead of leaning forward in the chair peering at the object the baby sat back and smiled. Mouth movements became more common. The 'proto reach' movements of the arms were replaced by small finger movements. In fact, we had got the kind of behaviour you expect when a baby is sitting in a chair opposite an adult involved in social communication. Further tests showed that the babies switched from one mode to the other when the movement of the stimuli objects changed from any simple or constant motion to a jerky or irregular movement. The only hypothesis that seems to explain these observations is that babies treat simple movements as those of inanimate objects while the irregular movements are treated as though they came from a living object that could be a potential social partner.

If babies do develop a difference reaction to people and things early on, this would be a useful skill to have in dealing with the world, because people and things tend to react in very different ways. If you do something to a physical object it usually reacts in a fairly simple way that reflects what has been done to it. If you push a ball on a flat surface it rolls or if you hit a hanging object it will swing. But people are not like this. The action–reaction cycle is much more complicated. If you stick your tongue out at an adult they might laugh or perhaps say something. Another social intelligence is interposed between the baby's action and the adult's response, or lack of it. The close analogue between the baby's action and the movement of a physical object is missing.

'The world is so full of a number of things . . .'

Imitation

Sometimes one or both the partners in a dialogue may attempt to do what the other one is doing—they imitate. But this is far from a simple reaction. You must perceive what the other person is doing and then translate this into a parallel movement of your

86

Can't get enough of it ...
Imitation as well as
muscular co-ordination
will ultimately result
in acceptable social
behaviour.

own. There have been long disputes among psychologists about the age at which babies begin to imitate. It is clear that in the first few months quite a lot of imitation does occur in adult–infant interactions but most of this is the adult imitating the baby. The early imitations of infants are restricted to a limited range of actions that are in the baby's social repertoire. Thus it is fairly easy to train a baby of a few months to stick out his tongue when you do the same but it is impossible at this age to get him to imitate your raising of your hand above your head or your blinking. It is perhaps better to consider these early 'imitations' as examples of the baby giving specific signals in defined social situations rather than true imitation. True imitation would involve some consciousness of doing the same thing as your partner and it seems unlikely that this occurs before the end of the first year.

Reciprocal exchange

Returning to the two modes of responding to people and to things; one way in which the mode of responding to people develops is by incorporating responses to objects into it. Before effective reaching is developed towards the middle of the first year this is done by the two responding to the same object by looking at it. The parent holds out an object for the baby to look at. The baby looks at the object and then at the parent. Perhaps the parent shakes the object and smiles. The baby looking at the object turns to the parent and smiles. Quite complicated games get built out of these kinds of sequences. Later when reaching is developed, give and take games become very common. Parents hand things to the baby who then hands them back. Some psychologists attach special importance to games like this which involve reciprocal exchange because exchange is such a basic feature of our social life.

Individual differences

By the latter part of infancy large individual differences are
apparent in reactions to people and things. Some infants are
happy to amuse themselves for long periods with a few objects to
manipulate while others quickly become bored with this kind of
activity and demand someone to play with. In the study
mentioned in chapter three of children who continued to wake
regularly at night beyond their first birthday, it was found that,
in general, these night waking children were happier playing
with objects than the babies that slept through the night. When
in a room with a parent these children were more likely to be
playing on their own with objects and spent less time in social

*Congenial company and
soothing sounds.
Novelty is important to
the developing
child's personality.*

Exploration of objects large and small is important for improving manual dexterity.

contact with the parent. They were less often taken out to play with other children. It is not clear why such differences arise. Perhaps the parents of these active night waking children are so exhausted by them that they cut down their social contact and the children adjust to this by spending more time playing with objects. Or it could be some more basic personality characteristic in the infants that tends to go together with the tendency to wake at night.

We know little of the long-term consequences of these kinds of individual differences. In broad terms they are unimportant. Certainly the object preferring children get enough social experience to develop all of the social skills and language in a quite normal way. When they are four-years-old they do get slightly better scores on IQ tests. This is probably because the tests used at this age contain quite a number of items that depend on manual dexterity and these children have probably had more practice at this kind of activity. But in the longer term they do not seem to have any particular educational advantage.

Limited value of games

The social games played in infancy again emphasise the adaptability of infants and the ways in which they are able to use widely differing experience to get to the same developmental goals. The major social skills emerge at roughly the same time in all children yet the kinds of social experience they have had to use to form these skills is very variable. There is a tendency for infants who have parents who talk to them a lot, and who play many social games with many different people to talk a little earlier but the effects are really very small. A reason for this is the dependency of the infant. The routine caretaking required to provide the basic needs, food, warmth, cleanliness and so on involves social interaction and social games. It may be less fun but a situation in which a baby is being persuaded to take some food is as valuable for social learning as any of the games described earlier. For this reason babies who get little play time develop their social competence at a very similar rate to those who get a lot of this experience.

7

Girls and boys: fathers and mothers

Throughout this book I have followed the usual convention and referred to babies as he, but, of course, almost half all babies are girls. In this chapter I want to consider those aspects of development which show a divergence between the two sexes and how the beginnings of a female or male gender identity can be seen in infancy. Gender identity can be defined as a person's image of themselves as a member of one or other sex. It is a social construction, an identity built within a social world, but it relates closely to a biological distinction: with very rare exceptions girls develop a female identity and boys a male one. Gender identity is a fundamental aspect of our lives. Test this out for yourself by trying to describe an imaginary person without making them male or female. It is virtually impossible. We think of everybody as individuals that are male or female. The same applies to ourselves. We live in the world as men or women and see it from one or other perspective.

In the social world there are a whole range of beliefs and expectations about how members of each gender behave and the social roles they occupy.[1] In the industrialised societies women are stereotyped as being passive, weak, submissive, intuitive and decorative while men are seen as aggressive, powerful, rational and independent. Of course, like any stereotypes these are not accurate descriptions or aspirations for many people, though in very broad terms they do fit the places the two genders occupy in the social system. Men almost always occupy the positions of power, prestige and responsibility while women predominate in the service and caring roles and, especially, are the major caretakers of children at home. Outside the home, most jobs in public health or education that deal with younger children are held by women. Increasingly these segregations of opportunity and expectation are being challenged and occasionally we find men who stay at home to look after children or who work in nurseries and women in the boardroom or the upper echelons of the trade unions. But we have a very long way to go before the aspirations of equal opportunity and status are fulfilled.

Parents are often guilty of reinforcing sex stereotypes by delineating specific roles not only for themselves but for their children as well.

Roles within the home are more complicated than in the world of employment. Women remain the major caretakers of children and domestic workers but they have also become much more important as wage earners outside the home with nearly half all women with children having paid employment in several countries.

A woman in the world of men—no longer a prisoner behind the kitchen sink.

The nineteenth-century (middle-class) father was a patriarch in the home as well as in society at large. He had custody of his (legitimate) children and control of all his wife's assets. She provided all the day to day needs of the children, where sufficiently affluent by the proxy of female servants, but otherwise her husband was firmly in control. These roles gave rise to the legal concepts of custody and care and control of children which still persist in England. Custody, which includes such matters as decisions about education, religion and marriage, represents the patriarchal authority while care and control are the daily activities carried out by women. The splitting of these functions was necessary because until the last half-century men almost always retained custody of their children after divorce, though the children would be looked after by the ex-wife or a female relation. Today, with the decline of patriarchy, both custody and care and control are generally given to the women.

Power gain

Despite continuing economic dependence for many wives, psychological power and control in the home has largely passed to them. This has come through growth of the idea of marriage as a reciprocal romantic attachment. Though there are still remnants of the earlier notion of a wife as a husband's property, most couples enter a marriage with a concept of equal but different roles. As the wife is generally the partner who spends most time in the house it is not surprising that she has gained power in the home, especially in matters to do with children.

This trend has been reinforced by new kinds of dynamics of relationship which have grown up between the isolated couples of the nuclear family. These are not always what you might expect from broader social roles of women and men in work and politics. A common domestic role for men is one of submission and subservience. They hide their angry and negative feelings (a continuation of the Victorian stiff upper lip) and try to buy off those of their partner by doing all they can to please. Dynamics like this can be very explosive. Women may be very frustrated by the lack of responses from their partner and may adopt more and more provocative behaviour. Eventually the husband's anger may surface and a clash becomes inevitable. The extraordinary dependency that men may have on their wives is thought to result from overexclusive relationships with their mothers in childhood. Fear of losing the all-providing mother inhibits the expression of frustration and anger. Adult life then becomes an unfulfilled search for an ever-giving mother-figure.

Area of controversy

In looking at the emergence of gender identity we must hold both the general and particular in mind; the ways in which child-rearing is formed and shaped by institutions and prevailing assumptions of society, and by the particular relationships a child forms with those immediately around him. The issues involved in a discussion of gender identity are deeply political. Roughly speaking we have two sides, the nativists, who believe that gender identity is fixed by biology and inevitable,[2] and the environmentalists, who see it as being produced by social conditioning. The first would argue, for instance, that it is a fact of biology that women are best fitted for the rearing of children and this is the principle aim and function of their lives. Thus their traditional role in the family is seen as natural and inevitable. Those on the other side would say that this role is neither natural nor inevitable, but the result of growing up in a society where a particular assumption about women's roles is heavily reinforced by many social institutions. To support this point of view they may well cite cases of other cultures where expectations and roles are different to show that other arrangements are possible. A nativist might try and counter this kind of evidence by suggesting that genetic differences between populations may account for the variation in behaviour.

Intellectual differences

Disputes between nativists and environmentalists are not confined to questions about gender identity and sex roles and have occurred over all aspects of behaviour that are of social relevance. Intelligence is another topic which has been much argued over in recent years. Like many such disputes in science, the answer is that both sides are wrong because the question is posed in a misleading way. It assumes that the outcome of development depends on two kinds of factors, biological givens or genes and the environment, which add together. On this view it would make sense to ask how much of each? We could assign percentages to the two kinds of factors, as has been done, and we then have a figure which is apparently a very precise answer to the nature–nuture question. However, the fallacy in this approach is that the two kinds of factors are not simply added together, they are intertwined and intermingled in the most complex way imaginable and this occurs at every step in the developmental process. A good analogy for the meaninglessness of the traditional nature–nuture question would be to ask how much of the area of a rectangle is due to its base and how much to its height. Of course to have an area it must have both. So it is with development, both a biological basis and an environment are required.

Given the complexity of the process we have no reason for thinking that development is either inevitable or unchangeable. The task of the developmental psychologists is to try and understand the processes involved. With this knowledge it should be possible to define the kinds of environment and child-rearing situations that are most likely to produce the outcomes that we believe are desirable.

In the case of sex differences in behaviour and gender identity we are seldom dealing with absolute differences. Women can do all things that men can and *vice versa*. Most differences that exist are small and are in average performance and in the probability of a member of one sex doing something. In the case of child-rearing, apart from breast-feeding, we have no reason to think that men and women are not both equally capable of doing anything. But under present social conditions women are more usually the major caretakers of children. Gender identities form early and will mean that children of each sex will relate somewhat differently to parents of each sex. So who looks after children will have some emotional consequences for children.

Sex differences in infancy

In terms of growth and indeed survival there are sex differences throughout fetal life and infancy. More boys than girls are conceived, but male fetuses are more often miscarried than female. Both perinatal deaths and those in the first year show an excess of males. The loss of males means that by the end of pregnancy there are about 105 males born to every 100 females. With the continuing slightly higher mortality for males an equal sex ratio is achieved in early adulthood and thereafter the proportion of females in the population steadily increases.

Not all the reasons for the mortality differential between the sexes are understood. The higher rates of male miscarriage may partly result from immunological problems. Male fetuses are genetically less like their mothers than female and this may result in rejection reactions which cause some to be miscarried. In the teenage years and early adulthood the higher mortality of men stems largely from accidents and therefore can be related to differences in living patterns. In Third World countries, female mortality in the middle years is higher because childbirth still carries a significant maternal mortality. But these factors do not explain the greater vulnerability of male children or shorter lifespan of men.

There are differences if we compare the birth weight and gestation length for the two sexes. Male newborns on average are slightly heavier than females, but they have a shorter gestation time. Like so many of the sex differences the margin is very small—we certainly cannot say that all male babies are larger— but in this instance are quite consistent.

Different treatment for boys and girls

When we turn to behavioural differences in early infancy we move to much more uncertain territory. Many sex differences have been reported in research studies, but equally often these results have been contradicted by later investigations.[3] It is quite possible that differences are not consistent. There are perhaps some conditions that accentuate differences while others minimise them. Given the wide divergences in the ways that infants are treated, such effects seem likely. What we can conclude with some certainty from all this is that sex differences in the behaviour of newborns are very small. Certainly nobody is going to be very successful if they try to tell the sex of babies from their behaviour.

You cannot do much better from the appearance and body build, assuming of course that the external genital region is concealed. Because our culture deals with people only as members of one or other sex steps are often taken to indicate the sex of a baby in the absence of other visible cues. Name labels appropriately coloured blue or pink are in wide use in hospitals as are coloured blankets. Parents, too, frequently mark the sex of their babies by their dress right from the moment of birth. Some studies, but by no means all, have shown that there are differences in the way mothers and fathers handle babies of each sex. Some of these differences are explained by a continuing preference for male children in industrialised cultures. While such preferences persist, differential treatment may stem from one sex being preferred, rather than a response related to the baby's sex itself. But the latter kind of effect also exists. Our notions of what is appropriate for boys or girls are extended to the newborn.

The most consistent finding of research studies, but again not a universal one in industrialised societies, is that boys are treated more physically, while girls receive more close affectionate contact and talking. Differences of this general kind have been reported throughout infancy. The inconsistency of such findings arise because the differences are always very small and therefore hard to measure, and because beliefs about how far children of each sex ought to be treated differently vary from place to place and across time as well as between individuals. At the present time the general trend is for parents to believe in equality of treatment during infancy.

What parents do with infants is not only a source of variation in their development but also arises, in part, from differences in infant behaviour. So throughout development we have the continuing influences of differential treatment of children of each sex by parents and everyone else the children may encounter and the effects on those people of behaviour that may differ between the sexes.

The gap widens

As babies grow up sex differences become more marked so that by the end of infancy, sex differences are consistent and quite striking. Girls begin to learn to speak before boys, so that if you take any phase of language development—say the production of the first recognisable word—this will occur, on average, three or four weeks earlier in girls. It is not understood why this should be. Some parents seem to talk more to their daughters than their sons and their talking may be more closely related to the child's activity and this could accelerate the development of speech. On the other hand, there is some evidence of an earlier maturation of some parts of the brains of girls. But this cannot be seen to be a simple 'cause' of the earlier talking, as the brain development could well be influenced by differing parental treatment of boys and girls or the uterine environment. Similarly, parents may talk more to girls because girl babies babble more.

Like all developmental problems everything seems to depend on everything else and it is very difficult or even impossible to say that there is any one simple cause of the difference. However, in a few cases this may be possible. Where one or other sex is consistently treated differently in a way that is known to influence behaviour, it may be possible to isolate this treatment as a cause of at least some behavioural effects. Male circumcision is a good example of such an effect.[4] In most industrialised countries male circumcision is dying out except where it is done to Jewish children for religious reasons. The decline is due to the decrediting of most of the supposed medical advantages of the surgery. However, in the United States the practice persists on a wide scale and in many hospitals as many as 80 per cent of all boys are circumcised in the first week of life. The operation is stressful to babies and probably painful and results in increased crying, disturbed sleep and wakefulness which may persist for a week or more. Clearly if the behaviour of samples of girl and boy

Jewish boys are circumcised on the eighth day of life. Do they feel pain and if so, to what extent is it traumatic?

babies are compared when the boys have just been circumcised, behavioural sex differences may well be found which are caused by the continuing effects of the circumcision. If this is the case we have an example of a sex difference which we can explain. In a society where most boys are circumcised we have a cultural belief that boys and girls should be treated differentially. Boys are subjected to a traumatic surgical procedure which may result in their behaving differently from girls. Assuming that circumcision is routinely carried out and its effects on behaviour are predictable we will have a consistent sex difference. In a case like this, the behavioural difference can, of course, be removed by ceasing to circumcise the boys.

Genital abnormalities

When a baby is born its sex is determined by the midwife, doctor or parents by looking at the external genital organs. If a penis is present the baby is announced to be a boy and is thereafter brought up as such. However, in a few very rare cases hormonal and other abnormalities can mean that the anatomy of the genitals gives a misleading indication of the child's true sex; the true sex being that shown by the chromosomes in each cell of the body.[5] In cases like this, children who are chromosomally one sex may be brought up as the other. Studies of such children show that the sex of assignment, what he is thought to be at birth and treated as during development, is of over-riding importance in determining how the child will behave. Generally speaking a child will behave like a member of the sex he or she is treated as during development, to a large extent regardless of the chromosomal (or biological) sex. So gender identity seems to be largely a product of the sex a child is treated as.

Children vary a good deal in the age at which they begin

97

Hard to tell whether I'm a boy or a girl ... Here's a tip. Turn back to p. 89 (right) for the answer.

consistently to refer to themselves as belonging to one gender, but the evidence points to fixing of a gender identity at a surprisingly early age. Part of the evidence for this comes from the study of children who, because of abnormalities, have been reared as the sex other than that shown by their chromosomes. When such mistakes are discovered it is usual to surgically correct the abnormalities of the genitals and change the child's sex to that of their chromosomes. If this is done before the age of two or three the transition is usually made fairly easily but at later ages there is often considerable psychological turmoil, suggesting that the gender identity is already fixed by this time.

Tentative self identification by gender certainly occurs before the close of infancy. The child begins to see himself as a boy or herself as a girl and identifies with adults and children of the same sex. The child begins to see that people (and animals) are divided into two camps of male and female and that people in each tend to behave in rather different ways. In a traditional family where the mother is at home looking after children and the father is out at work each day the growing child has a clear example of how the roles of men and women may differ. Identification with the appropriate parent begins the long process of building up a picture of the world from the perspective of a girl or boy.

Sexual stereotyping

This process is often seen in rather superficial terms and sometimes parents may assume that the worst aspects of stereotyping of sex roles can be avoided by not providing the typical 'sex appropriate' toys. But it seems unlikely that a girl's interest in dolls or a boy's in cars and tanks is simply determined by their toys. Much of what children do when they play consists of representations of what they see people doing in the world around them. If throughout childhood they are surrounded by examples of adults who do not confine themselves to the usual roles typical of their gender it might be possible to create a fundamental change in a person's view of what is appropriate. But, however much parents may modify their own behaviour in the home children still grow up in a world where at nursery and in early years at school teachers are almost always women, doctors are usually men and male nurses are rare. The effects of such a world are that parental attempts to reduce sexual stereotyping can only be partially successful. This is not to say that attempts to change things within the home are a waste of time. The example of fathers caretaking and women mending fuses and going out to work probably does open more possibilities to children and demonstrates to them that sex roles are socially determined and are not fixed for all time even in societies where stereotyping is predominant.

Learning a sex role

By a child's second birthday sex differences in behaviour are quite marked especially in situations where children from several homes are gathered together. In nurseries where a wide range of toys are available, it is probable that you will find the boys pushing cars around, playing chase or building towers of bricks, while the girls may be sitting at a table using paints or playing with dolls in the Wendy house. Girls too are more likely to be close to the (female) teacher and will more often talk to her.

Children, above all, are creatures intensely interested in social conduct. They watch others and then try things out for themselves. As they develop their awareness of their gender, they follow the patterns of their fellow members they see around them. This kind of identification is particularly strong between children of similar age, so in the latter phases of infancy when play with other children increases, opportunities for adopting the stereotyped behaviour often seen in nurseries increases.

Merging of sex roles in parents is desirable

In recent years fathers have tended to become more involved in the care of their children.[6] In so far as this has allowed infants to grow up with the idea that both women and men can provide caretaking and nurturing roles, it is likely to have an influence on gender identity despite all the counter-examples the children will find outside the home of traditional sex stereotypes. We have already seen the power of the first relationships with parents for shaping later attitudes and behaviour: there is every reason to think that this power extends to gender identity. An infancy and childhood in which both parents assume most aspects of both the traditional maternal and paternal role is likely to leave a child with a much richer sense of what is possible and desirable in later life as a girl or as a boy. This is one of the several reasons why most child psychologists welcome the movement towards more equal parental roles.

8 Learning to move and learning to think

Though the newborn can engage the world around him, he is largely an observer. He is dependent on others to move him around. In spite of his limited physical capabilities he is good at doing the things that are important to him, like sucking and swallowing and co-ordinating his head and eye movements. By the close of infancy things are very different. Most babies can walk, can hold and manipulate objects and have considerable capabilities for going out into the world and doing things for themselves. As physical capabilities develop, mental capabilities also grow, allowing the development of the new physical skills in an intelligent way.

Though walking or crawling are complex skills involving co-ordination of the movements of many muscles, their late appearance in human development is not because a long period of learning or practice is required. In many mammals such as horses or sheep the young are able to walk and run within minutes of birth. There is no reason to think that we could not do the same if evolutionary pressures had demanded it. But independent movement has a low priority in our timetable of development and there are good reasons why it should be delayed. As I have described earlier, the dependency of the human infant provides the means of developing into a social being. Lack of mobility ensures dependency and the learning of the social rules and skills essential for survival in a species with a complex culture. In fact, though we commonly talk of babies learning to walk, the development of walking does not involve learning and practice in the same sense as these are needed to become a competent football player or pianist. Infants are provided with varying opportunities for physical exercise and few receive specific lessons in walking, yet all of them, except those with rare abnormalities, successfully walk.

To run, to jump, to climb, to explore . . . The joys of gaining mastery over one's body.

Newborns can walk

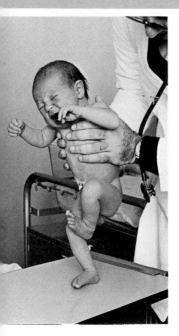

Far too young to walk—yet the newborn 'knows' the basic pattern of movement he will later need.

The basic pattern of co-ordinated movement required for walking is present in a newborn baby and can be easily demonstrated.[1] If a newborn is supported under the arms, leaning slightly forward with the soles of its feet first touching a firm surface, he will usually walk. Sometimes it is necessary to lightly stroke the top of one foot to get the first step and set the response off. Though the infant cannot, of course, support its own weight, these newborn stepping movements appear to be identical with those of a much older child who can walk independently. Some psychologists have argued that walking of newborns is not a reflex pattern (one set off by the brain without continuous feedback from the environment) because the stepping pattern seems to be adjusted to the surface the baby is walking on and that it is even possible to get babies to step over objects. Others are less convinced (try with your own baby and see what you think), but either way it is clear that the newborn 'knows' the basic pattern of movement required for walking. They can crawl too. If you put some support behind a baby's feet as he makes crawling movements he is able to push himself forward. The interesting thing about these early movement patterns is that they become difficult to elicit after a few months and are not seen again until the baby walks independently, usually sometime between nine and 18 months. This period of quiescence presumably results from the evolutionary pressures to increase the infant's dependence on his caretakers.

Average age for motor milestones

In the pre-war years much of the efforts of developmental psychologists in the United States has been more directed at establishing the time course of motor development. Large numbers of children were examined to establish the average age at which various points in development, the so-called motor milestones, were reached. Looking at the results of these studies tends to give the impression that the milestones represent a constant progression in development: sitting unsupported at six months, standing supported by furniture at eight-and-a-half months, walking alone at eleven-and-a-half months and so on.

However, there is great variability in the ages at which each stage is reached and even in the sequence of the stages. Walking, for instance, is quite normal at any time between nine months and 18 months. Crawling is similarly variable. For some children this is a very long stage lasting from the middle of the first year well into the second year, while for others it is very brief and they move quickly from sitting to standing and then walking. Other infants do not crawl at all but instead go through a phase of shuffling around on their bottoms. Though such children seem to walk later than others, these variations in the early locomotor patterns do not have long-term effects on development.

Variable rate

There are many reasons for the variability in the pattern of locomotor development. Particular patterns seem to run in families. I come from a family of early walkers. I walked at nine months, while my daughter took her first independent steps at eight-and-a-half months. It is tempting to label such effects as 'genetic' but no one has ever demonstrated genes associated with motor development. However, it is likely that many genes are involved in such a complex process and all sorts of other non-genetic factors which could well run in families are likely to be involved.

Some cultures, in East Africa for example, have been found to have accelerated motor development when compared to the norm in Europe or America. It has been suggested that this stems from genetic differences. However, the cultures that show the accelerated patterns tend to be ones where a good deal of stress is placed on physical development and it seems probable that such variations in caretaking styles may have a good deal to do with the rate of development.

Stimulation speeds it up

That specific encouragement and opportunity for movement can accelerate the development was demonstrated in the United States by Dr. Myrtle MacGraw.[2] She worked with a series of twins providing stimulation for only one of each pair. As the films she made testify, not only did the stimulated twin always reach the motor milestones earlier, but she was able to produce quite remarkable physical skills and competence at very early ages. One of her more dramatic film sequences shows a two-year-old roller skating with an assurance and skill that many adults never achieve. At the other extreme we have the example of Navajo children who spend much of the first year strapped to a cradleboard (see chapter three), yet walk independently at a slightly earlier average age than white American children. These experiments are yet another testament to the adaptability of the human infant. They also show that, though specific instruction and teaching is not required to develop the human 'universals' like walking and that children provide their own environment for development, giving specific stimulation and encouragement can speed up the process.

With specific instruction and practice, physical skills which are not universally developed can be taught at surprisingly early ages. Swimming is a good example. A newborn will make 'dog paddle' movements if suspended in water and will raise his head to keep his nose clear. If given frequent practice it is possible to get children swimming quite effectively by the second half of the first year and thereafter they will gain in skill and confidence. In the first year most infants do not show any fear of water and many of them seem to derive a lot of enjoyment from splashing around in the bath or swimming pool (with adult support). If swimming is encouraged at this time, the pleasure derived from water usually persists throughout childhood. However, if

Bottom in the air and the world is upside down ... Stand right-side-up— Oops! It's bottom on the ground.

The young baby has no fear of water and can often be taught to swim (or sink) before his first birthday.

swimming practice is not given in the first year a fear of water seems to set in and it is then often difficult to teach a child to swim until they are six- or seven-years-old.

Reaching and grasping

The finer grade hand and finger movements involved in grasping and reaching follow the same kind of pattern of development as locomotor movements. Under suitable conditions, a newborn can orientate his arms towards an interesting object. Hands and fingers often point towards an object quite accurately and crude hitting movements may be made. If the object is in range, a hit may be scored but the infant cannot grasp the object as the opening and closing of the hand is not co-ordinated with the swipe. Grasping is possible at this age but only when an object is placed in the palm of the baby's hand.

Controlled reaching and grasping of objects does not usually occur until towards the middle of the first year, but frequent practice in swiping at things and grasping do seem to accelerate the development. The 'delay' in the appearance of visually guided reaching has been attributed to the complexity of putting together the accurate visual perception system needed for such movements with the close co-ordination of movement of the muscles of the arm and hand. However, given the newborn's abilities for orientation in space and co-ordination of complex muscle movements for activities like sucking, there is little doubt that this development could take place much earlier if evolutionary pressures had demanded it. Like locomotion, we may assume that it is not a priority during the first phase of total dependence in early infancy. By the second half of the first year reaching does become important, not least in social games. The offering and exchange of objects with social partners becomes a very significant part of an infant's social encounters at this time. Such games help to focus the attention of infant and adult on the same object and this may be important in the first stages of speech because it ensures that both are 'talking' about the same thing.

Grasping a fascinating foot seems simple enough—yet it takes accuracy of visual perception and co-ordinated movement.

Piaget's theories

In the past the development of motor skills has often been considered rather separately from the growth of mental abilities but in recent years we have begun to understand how closely the two are tied together. In fact, many psychologists would see this joint and co-ordinated development as being the major task of infancy. Very influential in the formation of this viewpoint have been the theories of Jean Piaget.[3]

Piaget has been concerned with the theoretical description of the way a child conceptualises a view of the world and his actions in it. He is an epistemologist—one who studies knowledge in this very broad sense. Over a lifetime's work, beginning with observations of his own children, he has built up a comprehensive theory of development from birth to adulthood.

'I am the world and the world is me ...'
To this infant, mother's face is just an extension of himself.

Totally egocentric

Piaget calls infancy the sensory–motor period, thus emphasising the infant's preoccupation with the co-ordination of sensory perception and motor activity and the lack of complex mental images of the world. Piaget assumes that at birth the infant is totally *egocentric*. He is unable to make any distinction between himself and the rest of the world. He does not know that he or anything else exists. His own movements and things that impinge on him coming in from the outside world all seem one to him. By the end of the sensor–motor period (the end of infancy) a clear distinction between himself and his own actions and the world outside has been made. Or in other terms, he has now constructed a model of the world in his head which allows him to recognise familiar objects and, importantly in Piaget's theory, he knows that objects will continue to exist even when he cannot see or feel them. This development is achieved by the infant actively working on the world by looking at it and moving in it. It is a continuous process of the infant adapting to the world outside and using that world to increase his knowledge of it and the way he can act on it.

Piaget conceptualises this process with his terms, assimilation and accommodation. Assimilation consists of taking in knowledge about the world and making it fit into the infant's existing knowledge or model of the world. Piaget uses the analogy of eating for this process where food is brought into the body and made part of it. In order to deal effectively with the world, the child also needs to be able to alter his behaviour to fit outside conditions. This is accommodation. Assimilation and accommodation are the two sides of the same coin and occur continuously as the infant begins to act in the world. The continuing struggle to reach an equilibrium with the environment with these dual processes, provides the spur that pushes cognitive development on to more complex levels of structures.

Hide and seek

In Piaget's theory, one of the most important stages in the sensor–motor period is the achievement of object permanence: the point when the infant realises that an object continues to exist even when it cannot be seen. In his original experiment, Piaget demonstrated this by hiding an object his child was playing with under a cushion. Before about seven months the infant would not look for the object when it was hidden. He seemed to lose all interest in it; or in terms of the theory, it ceased to exist for him. But after this age the behaviour was quite different. The infant would continue to search for the object and would remove the cushion to find it.

Later in the sensor–motor period Piaget describes the separation of mean and ends. This is the point where the infant's mental model of the world is sufficiently detailed for him to seek different ways of achieving the same goal. If he cannot reach a desired object with his hand he may pick something up which he can use to knock the object towards himself. He has become a tool user and one that is not solely dependent on trial and error because he can use his mental representation of the world to solve problems. The sensor–motor comes to the end with the emergence of symbolic functioning. When signs and symbols can stand for objects not only is language possible, but much more complex problems can be solved in the period when signs and symbols can be manipulated rather than the object themselves.

At the present time Piaget's theories are under intense debate.[4] Further work has modified many of the details—for instance, the exact way in which an object is hidden seems to influence the age at which object permanence can be seen. But the great virtue of the theory is that it does emphasise the positive role the infant plays in his development. Cognitive development occurs because the infant acts on the world. Its weakness is that it confines itself to cognition, 'cold blooded cognition' some have said, and pays little attention to the infant's social world. It is not simply that the principles are not applied to social situations, but it fails to emphasise that social world is the cradle of language and thought.

Many of the steps in development which are crucial to Piaget first emerge in the course of the infant's day-to-day social life. For instance, one can talk of people permanence as well as object permanence. At what age does the infant respond to the disappearance and reappearance of a familiar person in a way that suggests he can in some sense hold a picture of that person in his head? The usual answer seems to be rather earlier than he will search for an object that is hidden by a cushion. Indeed studies of social responsiveness suggest that it is through the daily encounters with his caretakers that he learns the principle of the continuing existence of people or objects separate from himself and so begins the process of seeing himself as separate from the world. Games like peek-a-boo may form an important learning situation for this vital step in development.

Intelligence tests

While Piaget was concerned with the general process of development as seen in all individuals, many other psychologists have concentrated on the difference between individuals and the question of the prediction of future performance from such variation.[5] Intelligence tests are the well known example of this kind of approach. A test is constructed by taking questions which seem to reflect the ability we are interested in (intelligence) and trying them out on groups of children. An age level is then set for each question on the basis of this preliminary testing. This is the age at which half the children in a broadly based sample will be able to answer the question correctly. Working in this way a collection of questions is built up which sample the ability we are concerned with and cover the age span we require. For most IQ tests this is about four to 16 years or to adulthood. To test an individual, questioning is begun at a level below the child's age and is continued until there is a run of questions the child cannot answer correctly. From the highest level questions answered correctly the child's mental age is derived. This is then converted into an IQ by the simple formula:

$$IQ = \frac{\text{mental age}}{\text{chronological age}} \times 100.$$

So if a child is aged ten but can answer questions up to the twelve-year-old mental age level the IQ is 120—i.e. IQ = 12/10 × 100. Conversely, if the child can only reach the nine-year-old level, the IQ is 90.

What we need to notice about tests of this kind is that the child being tested is compared with other children and that the intelligence quotient is an expression of that child's performance relative to the larger sample. Furthermore the construction of the test embodies the developmental assumption that as children get older they will be able to answer an increasing number of questions. Indeed IQ is really a plot of question-answering ability (of the kind included in the test) against age. When we say that a child has a high IQ we mean that he or she is able to answer questions that, on average, we would only expect to be answered successfully by an older child. A low IQ means that the child is unable to answer questions that an average ability child of the same age could manage.

'How does the fish breathe in there . . .?' Each day, his inquiring mind adds to its store of knowledge. The amount he has absorbed and his ability to verbalise it are reflected in his IQ score.

When IQ is being used to predict future performance we are assuming that a child who is able to answer questions above or below his age level will continue to show superior or inferior abilities as compared with other children in the future. So, in effect, we are defining ability as the rate of progress in development.

Consistency of performance

Over the school years this assumption seems to work quite well. That is to say, children who do well in school work and on IQ tests early in their career are likely to be doing well several years later. There are several reasons for this consistency. Partly it is because the developmental assumption embodied in the tests is at least partially correct. Over the range of abilities reflected in an IQ test, rate of increase in ability seems fairly consistent so that a child who is a year ahead at age five is quite likely to be a year ahead at age seven. A second reason is that selective school systems and teachers' attitudes tend to reinforce the consistency of children by streaming and by setting up expectations. Studies of children, who before selection are borderline in performance between high and low ability streams, shows that their subsequent performance on tests or in the classroom tends to resemble that of their class mates. So the test scores of the borderline children who are put into the high ability stream tends to rise, while those of children going into the low ability group tends to fall.

Manual dexterity is an important feature of intelligence tests for children.

An early walker perhaps—but this does not necessarily mean that he will fare well in later IQ tests.

A final factor working towards consistency of performance over age is the children's home background. There is much evidence that the home has an important influence on school

performance and IQ test results. Normally, of course, it is a constant influence so that it will tend to keep the child at the same level of performance relative to his peers. All this means that IQ or school performance is not just a result of the amount or quality of grey matter in a child's head, it also depends a good deal on what goes on around him. When the environment changes, IQ is likely to change too. Often if we look at the lives of children whose IQ have shown a change we can find events that may account for it—a divorce or change of school, perhaps.

Development quotient

The general principles of infant testing follow those of intelligence tests. Such tests are usually called developmental tests and the quotient is called a DQ or developmental quotient. Instead of questions, the tester assesses such things as locomotor development, manipulation of objects and social responses. Each item in the test is given an age level and the DQ is calculated in just the same way as an IQ.

Dad may have high hopes for his child's sporting prowess—but it is still impossible to predict the boy's future abilities.

If we look at the predictive power of developmental tests we find that it is very low. But given that an infant is a very different creature from a school child, this is hardly very surprising. Remembering the analogy I used earlier of insect development I think it is easy to understand this. Suppose we were asked to assess caterpillars and predict the performance of butterflies. Would we necessarily expect the caterpillars which reached their maximum body-size first to metamorphose into the furthest flying butterflies or even the fastest crawling caterpillars to be the fastest flying butterflies?

110

What is the significance of test results?

When we talk of the predictive power of DQ tests we usually mean do DQs predict IQs? The answer is no, because the items in DQ tests are very unlike those in IQ tests. Should we expect that a child who is somewhat early in crawling and walking to be especially good at answering the verbal questions that tend to predominate in IQ tests? Unless we have good evidence that all aspects of development tend to go in close parallel—which we do not—and that the rate of development or passing of the milestones is an important indicator of later performance we should not expect the prediction to be very good. Even if we confine ourselves to specific aspects of development the associations are not much better. For instance, children who show accelerated motor development do not seem to be especially gifted in athletics in later life. So the basic assumption that rate in early development is connected to later performance does not seem to be a general principle. Indeed, on an evolutionary level it would be odd if this were true, given the arguments I have set out earlier for the advantages of an extended period of dependency. If extended dependency is important for the acquisition of important social and cognitive skills, we would not expect early autonomy to be highly associated with later above average social and cognitive skills.

Interestingly enough, as we get towards the end of infancy when the DQ test begins to include items that closely resemble IQ questions, we do find some predictive power. This becomes true when verbal items begin to figure in the DQ test.

The lack of predictive power in DQ tests does not mean that all prediction from infancy is impossible. First of all, given the importance of the social world in development, you can make quite accurate predictions for things like school performance, IQ and even eventual employment from information about the infant's parents. The average of an infant's parents IQs is a better prediction of the infant's IQ than any test you can do on the infant himself for five or six years. Of course, predictions of this kind assume that the infant is intact and will develop normally and that the developmental environment will not undergo any dramatic upheavals.

Handicapped infants

At an individual level some prediction is possible by the recognition of abnormality. Where a baby is born with a known handicapping condition some sort of informed guesses about possible futures can be made on the basis of the knowledge of development of similar children. In essence, this is what a paediatrician does when he or she assesses a child with a developmental handicap. However, it should not be thought that just because a diagnostic label can be given to a child, a very

111

precise prediction about outcome can be made. All the variety of factors which influence normal children also effect the development of those with abnormalities. In fact, outcome is more variable for handicapped children partly because for them specific teaching or training may be necessary to learn what a normal child could achieve by their own efforts in any reasonable environment. For instance, children who are born blind or become blind as young infants (once a relatively common complication for preterm babies who were given excess oxygen while in an incubator) often show delayed and abnormal speech patterns. Subsequent research has suggested that these difficulties stem from the limited social interaction these children often have in infancy. Blind babies tend to be rather unresponsive and do not provide much of the social stimulation that parents and others get from normal children. They turn their parents off. However, if parents understand these processes and have plenty of emotional support in their very difficult situation, many of these effects can be avoided and the child's speech is relatively normal. Blind children provide a vivid illustration of the idea that infants play a very active part in their own development by creating their own psychological world. Where a child is damaged these processes are interrupted and special steps have to be taken to provide what the infant cannot create for himself.

A blind child's sense of the world can be promoted by helping him to 'see' through the eyes of his parents.

Mongolism

Some developmental abnormalities have multiple effects on the child's progress. Down's Syndrome or mongolism illustrates this. This abnormality is caused by an extra chromosome and is recognisable at birth by characteristic creases in the skin on the palm of the hand and the soles of the feet. The extra chromosome influences brain development so that these children tend to have quite low intelligence, though the range is wide. The ultimate level of performance does depend on the developmental environment. Down's children remaining at home, for instance, tend to do better than those who go to an institution, especially if they are institutionalised early in development and the institution is one that is large and run on traditional lines.

The processes for controlling muscle movements are impaired in these children and they are often very floppy as babies and may be rather clumsy and have a slouching posture later on. Heart defects are also common and these together with an increased vulnerability to chest infections means that the life expectations of these children is relatively short. The use of antibiotics and often medical technologies has extended their lifespan but it is still unusual for them to survive beyond early adulthood.

Early intervention

In recent years systems of developmental assessment have been set up in many communities. These are designed to find children with either specific syndromes or those with non specific abnormalities that might benefit from some kind of intervention or special education. For some conditions early intervention may prevent the development of abnormalities, which once present are very difficult or impossible to correct. Deafness is a good example. As deaf children cannot hear speech, they cannot learn to speak themselves. But the ease of language acquisition after the provision of a hearing aid depends greatly on age. If a hearing aid is given before a year or 18 months, speech may well develop relatively normally. However, if the aid is given later speech may show many peculiarities which can persist for a lifetime. It appears that there is a 'sensitive period' for language acquisition after which learning becomes much more difficult.

This idea is confirmed by studies of children who have suffered injuries to their brain. Even quite severe injuries suffered in the first couple of years may have mild long-term effects whereas the same injury at a later age can cause a permanent impairment. At the earlier ages the brain is still plastic so that after injury functions can be taken over by the intact areas. But as development proceeds, the brain becomes set in its patterns, so that this compensation process is less and less efficient.

This early ability to compensate after injury and make good losses of function is another reason why prediction is difficult from infancy. It emphasises once again that infants, despite their apparent vulnerability, are very tough in some ways because developmental processes can reach common goals in alternative ways. As adults we may be better at using our wits to minimise the effects of damage or hostile environments, but our capacities for biological compensation are more limited than those of babies.

9 The end of infancy

By the end of infancy—towards the end of the second year—the child has become a very different creature from the newborn baby. Most striking perhaps is the ability to talk and to move around independently from adults. More subtle, but no less dramatic, are the autonomy of action (the ability to originate plans and carry them through) and the understanding of social situations and meanings expressed both through words and non-verbally. It is a remarkable biological and social feat that in a few short months such fundamental change can take place. The infant has completed the first great step to adulthood, because by the close of infancy he is a member of his culture as he can speak and be understood and he can play a small but independent part in his social life.

Though the ability to speak marks the *end* of infancy, it is during this period that all the foundations for this remarkable achievement are laid. So in this final chapter I will discuss the acquisition of language.

Language learning

The study of child language has been one of the most active and exciting parts of developmental psychology in the past decade and ideas about the processes involved have undergone a major revolution. The major stimulus for this came from the work of the American linguist, Noam Chomsky.[1] To understand his ideas we need first to look at the theory that was most likely held before Chomsky put forward his ideas in the early 1960s.

Before this time the general belief was that children learnt language by a number of processes that were common to the learning of many other things. The most important of these were association, which is the perceiving of a connection between two events often occurring at the same time, reward, punishment and imitation. It was supposed that the babbling noises made by infants in the first year are associated by them with various pleasant sensations, like food, warmth and body contact, which are provided by the adult. The more noises infants make, the more adult attention they receive. Adults are most likely to respond to infant babbling when the noises resemble human speech sounds, so gradually infants come to make noises of this

'He says I'm still a baby!'

kind. Vocabulary was thought to be learnt by association. The infant frequently hears the name of an object when it is visible or being used and in this way begins to learn the names of things, actions and adjectives. More complicated grammatical structures were thought to be learnt by imitation and by reward and punishment. It was assumed that parents give a child reinforcement when they utter a correct sentence, while incorrect grammar is pointed out and corrected. All these processes were well known and have been widely demonstrated in the learning of other skills, so it seemed a reasonable assumption that they could account for the learning of language. Indeed, recent research suggests that they are all involved, but we now believe that they are necessary but in no way sufficient to account for language learning.

In the 1950s there were doubts about the then-current theory (perhaps too grand a name) of language learning. In particular, it seemed remarkable that reward and punishment and association were powerful enough to account for the very rapid development of speech. However, in the absence of any better ideas, accounts in these terms were duly repeated in all the text books.

New theory

Chomsky first made his name by writing a devastating critique of one version of this kind of theory. In essence he showed that principles of this kind just didn't fit the facts. He pointed out that children use incorrect sentences and forms of words that they can have seldom, if ever, heard. Moreover, similar mistakes are made by all children. Examples of this are the attempts to give an irregular verb a regular form—'goed' for 'went' or 'speaked' for 'spoken' or the addition of an 's' to make the plural of an already plural noun—'childrens', 'geeses'. Chomsky pointed out that the frequency of errors of this kind suggested that children were not basing their learning on associationalist principles but on rule learning. They appeared to acquire rules about language which they then applied (not consciously, of course) to new words or sentence constructions. Many errors occurred because the first rules that children acquire are overgeneralised and take no account of the exceptions and irregular forms.

Chomsky proceeded to describe the rules that are necessary for specifying the structure of all correct sentences, what is called a 'generative grammar'. He argued that at this abstract level all languages share a set of basic universal rules and suggested that the reason why children seemed so efficient at learning to speak was that they were born with a predisposition to understand these universal rules. This was generally known as a 'language acquisition device'. It was assumed that as infants heard speech from adults they could use this device to understand its structure in abstract terms and gradually use this knowledge to develop the more specific and complex rules required for speaking the particular language they heard. It was not claimed that children were predisposed to learn any particular language, as it is well known that all children seem to have an equal capacity to learn whatever language happens to be spoken around them. Rather they were thought to have a device which gave them the general structure of any language that they could use to learn the particular language they heard.

Chomsky's ideas were very influential because they introduced the idea that children learn language via generalised rules and this opened up a whole new field of study. Much research effort was directed at recording what children said at each stage of language acquisition, and describing this in terms of the grammatical rules involved, so that the elaboration of these through development could be traced. However, almost all this effort was directed at syntax (the structural properties of language or grammar) and very little attention was paid to semantics (meaning) or the social rules that governed the actual use or effects of speech. Increasingly it was pointed out that there was much more to language acquisition than syntax. Children somehow had to learn what words meant, not merely how to combine them into grammatically correct sentences. In addition, they also learn a great deal about how and when to use language, issues that were almost completely ignored in Chomsky's theories.

Infant social life

Learning the rules of social behaviour— perhaps an early rehearsal for a boardroom encounter?

Today the emphasis in research on language acquisition has tended to shift away from the grammatical analysis of what children say, towards the study of how what they say is related to social situations.[2] Though most would agree that babies are born with specific abilities to acquire language, the language acquisition device is seen less as a bit of machinery in the child's mind and more as part of the social encounters of infancy. Studies of infant social interactions have been brought together with

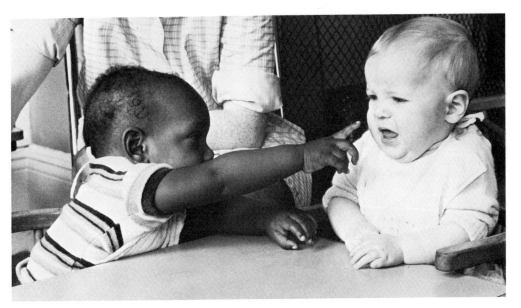

those of child language and we have begun to see language as a special case, and a very important one, of learning about the social world. Learning about the social world involves the learning of rules of conduct: these are not simply rules for correct behaviour in the sense of what is morally right or wrong, but much more generally about how to conduct all everyday social encounters.

We see the infant very much as a rule-learning creature, observing the social behaviour of others, trying it out himself and so absorbing principles of social life. I think anybody who has spent a lot of time with older infants must have been struck by their sense of occasion; their ability to associate particular activities with particular times and places. Often this can be seen in the form of frequently repeated rituals. When they visit a particular house they may always ask to be allowed to ring the door bell or may ask for some special food or toy. At its most fundamental social life can be reduced to a set of repeated actions of this kind and much of an infant's energies go into acquiring and performing them. Knowing what to say and when to say it may well be learned in the same way and indeed may develop out of the infant's understanding of the rules of social encounters.

Full circle

In a funny way our understanding of language learning has come a full circle. In the pre-Chomsky days the learning of language was thought to involve the same associationalist principles that were then thought to be involved in all other social learning. Then Chomsky came along and argued that language learning was very special and different and was essentially rule-learning based on some general rules the babies were born with (the language acquisition device). At the same time psychologists who investigated the development of social behaviour were finding that the associationalist ideas did not seem to work for these aspects of behaviour any better than they did for language and they began to suggest that social behaviours developed through rule learning. So once again we are back in the position where we believe that language learning operates on the same general principles as more general learning about the social world but now it is thought that both involve the acquisition of general rules or principles, not association.

Starting to speak

It would be an exaggeration to say that we understand how children learn to speak but the recent flurry of activity of developmental psychologists and linguists seems to have established the broad line of what is involved.

Our first assumption has to be that a baby is born with a predisposition to learn to speak, just as it is predisposed to become a member of a social species with a culture. We do not know all that is involved in this predisposition but the ability to enter into reciprocal social interchange is likely to be at the heart of it. At first much of the structure of social interactions is provided by the parent. They respond in predictable ways to what the infant does, but gradually the infant begins to play a more active part and some of the initiative begins to pass to him. This is possible because he begins to try and make sense of his social world by searching out the regularities—the rules. But this is not something done consciously: the infant finds that if he responds in certain ways to adults they respond in particular ways to him. So the simple smiling games and peek-a-boo evolve. Already in these early encounters the foundations of language are being laid. Not

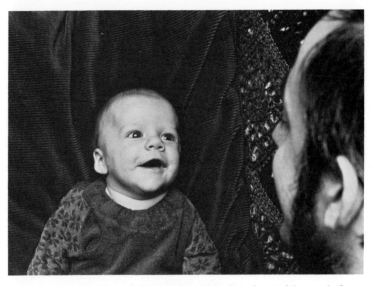

Words play no part in this engrossing interaction which will lay the foundations of language.

only do they involve rule learning but already at this age infants begin to pay attention to speech and respond to the speech sounds that adults make. This selective attention to speech sounds is another part of the potential for language learning that an infant has at birth. Of course, the infant does not understand what the parent says, but by association begins to learn something of the meaning of particular tones of voice and inflexions. Quite young babies, for instance, become upset and may cry when people near them become angry and raise their voices. He finds that adults respond to noises he makes and that this happens most effectively when his noises come at particular points in social encounters. At this stage the emphasis is much more on when you say things than what you say.

Baby talk

When people talk to infants their speech changes in certain characteristic ways from the way they talk to older children or adults.[3] Their sentences tend to be short and to have a very simple structure. They seldom, for instance use embedded clauses or passives. Words and phrases are often repeated and the total size of the vocabulary is small. The pitch of the voice is higher than usual, intonation is more varied and there is a greater frequency range. These features of talk to infants seem to be found in all cultures and can be noticed when quite young children as well as adults talk to babies. There are several probable reasons for them. An obvious one is that people do not have a lot to say to babies. Normally we do not try to convey complex ideas to them. Often we are simply affirming our presence as a social partner, we are communicating for the sake of communication, not because we have a vital message.

This is the cradle of communication in which the infant begins to learn about the social world he has been born in, while his parents and others begin to show him in simplified form the ways of that world. This modified speech to infants provides them with an ideal environment for learning these ways and shows several parallels with non-verbal communication. This too shows simplifications and exaggerated features when it is directed to infants. Films of adults interacting with babies have an odd slow and deliberate look. Gestures are clearer and easier to understand than those seen in adult-to-adult encounters. The simplifications and repetitions are likely to make rule-learning easier while the

Gesture and action are their main means of communication—and they'll understand mother's displeasure by the tone of her voice.

exaggerations and emphasis help to hold the attention of the infant. The modifications of both speech and non verbal gestures make social encounters both more interesting and more predictable and understandable. As infancy progresses the baby's growing understanding allows the development of larger and more complex interactions. At the same time his growing understanding provides both the need and the means for conveying more elaborate feelings and messages. The infant has more to say but still has to convey it by gesture and action, not words.

First words

But as the end of the first year approaches the infant produces his first recognisable word. Very often this is the name of one of the more significant figures in his social world.[4] At first words are produced as if they were a sort of optional extra to the social understanding that is created through gesture and non-language sounds. The first words do not carry any extra meaning for the adults. The words are usually spoken in the presence of the object or person to which they refer. However, they are important to the adult who usually sees them as a landmark in development and they provide a great stimulus for further social exchanges. Gradually the infant's words do begin to add a new dimension to his dealings with adults. He begins to refer to things that are not present, perhaps an object he wants or a person who is absent. At this point, though his command of language is still extremely limited, he has made the first faltering step as a member of his culture. He has used language to extend his communication beyond the here-and-now. That is the essence of a culture. We live in a culture where we can discuss the past and the future and entirely imaginary worlds. It is language that makes this possible and as an infant acquires language he enters that world.

But while an infant is in the single word stage the meaning he attaches to words may be very different to the conventions of adulthood. 'Cat' may mean any animal with fur and four legs or 'mama' is used to refer to any adult who seems likely to offer assistance. Quite frequently the meaning of a word goes through a three stage evolution. At first it is used very specifically; 'boy' used only to refer to the infant's brother. Then it is generalised very widely so it becomes a word for all children and finally the meaning is narrowed down to the usually accepted adult meaning.

Knowing what a baby intends when he utters a word is a complex question. If an infant says 'cat' is he saying 'there is a cat', 'where is the cat?' or 'I want the cat'? To the adults who know him the meaning is often clear from the general context of what is going on as well as their past joint experience. In fact, it may well be a mistake to always try to place too precise a meaning on what the child says at this stage. As with earlier non-verbal communication the point may be more to enter into a conversation and to keep adults talking than to convey a precise wish. The child's speech also has an experimental quality in which he is trying out the effects of saying things. But increasingly speech is used for specific effects—a repeated cry of 'milk, milk' may not cease until the child is given some milk.

Conveying a meaning

Often the child stays in the single word stage for several months. New words are added to the vocabulary and words are used with increasingly precise and adult-like meaning. But even though the grammatical complexity of what is said does not seem to change—the child has not yet begun to combine words into primitive sentences—the child's understanding of and control of social encounters increases steadily.[5] Quite complex verbal instructions, 'Your bottle is on the table', are understood and acted on long before the child says things of similar complexity. But often even with single words and a lot of help from his parents' knowledge of him he can convey what he wants effectively. So saying 'bottle' in a questioning or insistent tone will bring the reply 'your bottle is on the table' and the child goes to find it successfully. A child can ask for help without any words at all. An object is stuck in the opening of the posting box. Holding it up for a parent is often enough to have it removed. Actions of this kind emphasise how much the child's social understanding has advanced. Soon words begin to be combined in pairs and very soon after that more complicated phrases and then infancy has ended.

Which comes first: thought or language?

There is a long-standing debate among psychologists about whether thought precedes language or *vice versa*.[6] The answer seems to be that the two go hand in hand. Without thought you cannot speak. At least, without the capacity to hold mental images of the world in your head, speech is impossible. So obviously a child must be beyond Piaget's object permanence stage before speaking. But at the same time the advent of speech

Now it's just a feeling of sheer, simple pleasure. Later, he'll be able to think about it and eventually to convey it in words.

seems to allow more complicated thought and the ability to solve problems without acting them out on objects in the world. Imagination only flowers after language acquisition has proceeded some way, or so it appears. But appearances may be a bit deceptive. Watching a child at the one-word stage you cannot but be impressed by his command and understanding of the social world. In a familiar environment with familiar people he seems to understand quite subtle changes in mood of those around him and plays complicated games. His means of expression, however, are still limited and how are we to know all of what goes on in his head? Perhaps his imaginative powers are much more sophisticated than we customarily believe. Watching children play gives some hints that already at this age they have the power to turn bricks into cars and shoes into boats.

Time to move on

In eighteen months or so the newborn becomes a toddler and so leaves infancy and enters into the next stage of childhood. Never again in a lifetime will the rate of change be so fast or new skills and abilities arrive so quickly. As their child leaves this first phase, parents are likely to have mixed feelings. The newly found expressiveness and autonomy bring new possibilities and rewards in daily life and the endless days and nights of unremitting cleaning and feeding begin to retreat a little as they are relieved by moments of almost adult-like behaviour. But at the same time most of us have some feelings of regret. There is a very deep satisfaction for most parents in being able to hold and (occasionally) comfort an entirely dependent baby. But we have to move on with our own children though the experience of those first weeks and months always stays with us.

No longer a baby—time now to discover the expanding horizons of childhood.

References

1   Birth and after

1. Though I am aware that nearly half all babies are girls, I will follow convention
   and refer to them all as he except where my remarks apply specifically to girls.
   The alternative of using she as a general pronoun makes for confusion
   between babies and their mothers while the constant use of she/he and him or
   her seems unnecessarily clumsy.
2. Chard, T. and Richards, M. P. M. (Eds.). *Benefits and Hazards of the New
   Obstetrics. Clinics in Developmental Medicine No. 64.* London/Philadelphia:
   Heinemann Medical Books/Lippincott, 1977.
   Kitzinger, S. and Davis, J. (Eds.). *The Place of Birth.* London: Oxford University
   Press, 1978.
3. Klaus, M. H. and Kennell, J. H. *Maternal–infant Bonding.* St. Louis: Mosby,
   1976.
4. Brimblecombe, F. S. W., Richards, M. P. M. and Roberton, N. C. R. (Eds.).
   *Separation and Special-care Baby Units. Clinics in Developmental Medicine No.
   68.* London/Philadelphia: Heinemann Medical Books/Lippincott, 1978.
5. Winnicott, D. W. *The Child, the Family and the Outside World.* London: Penguin,
   1964.

2   Growth and feeding

1. Chamberlain, R., Chamberlain, G., Howlett, B. and Claireaux, A. *British Births
   1970. Vol. 1.* London: Heinemann Medical Books, 1975.
2. See Chamberlain et al., above and Butler, N. R. and Bonham, D. G. *Perinatal
   Mortality.* Edinburgh: Livingstone, 1963.
3. Kretchmer, N., Rossi, E. and Sereni, F. *Milk and Lactation.* Basel: Karger, 1975.
4. Le Leche International. *The Womanly Art of Breastfeeding.* NY: Tandem, 1970.
5. Leiderman, P. H., Tulkin, S. R. and Rosenfeld, A. *Culture and Infancy.*
   London/NY: Academic Press, 1977.
6. Erikson, E. H. *Childhood and Society.* London: Penguin, 1964.

3   Sleeping and crying

1. Bernal, J. F. 'Night waking in infants during the first 14 months.' *Developm.
   Med-child Neurol.* 1973, **15**, 760–769.
2. Emde, R. N., Walker, S. 'Longitudinal study of infant sleep.' *Psychophysiology*,
   1976, **13**, 456–471.
   Roffwark, H. P., Muzio, J. N. and Dement, W. C. 'Ontogenic development of the
   human sleep–dream cycle.' *Science*, 1966, **152**, 608–610.
   Dunn, J. *Distress and Comfort.* London: Open Books/Fontana, 1977.
3. Bridger, W. H. 'Sensory habituation and discrimination in the human neonate.'
   Amer. J. Psychiat., 1961, **117**, 991–996.
4. Chisholm, J. S. and Richards, M. P. M. 'Swaddling, cradleboards and the
   development of children'. *Early Human Development*, 1978, **3**, 255–275.

4   What can newborns do?

1. Bowlby, J. *Attachment and Loss. Vol. 1. Attachment.* London: Hogarth
   Press/Penguin, 1969.
2. Haith, M. M. 'Visual Competence in Early Infancy'. In R. Held, H. Liebowitz
   and H. R. Teuber (eds.) *Handbook of Sensory Physiology. Vol. 8.* Berlin:
   Springer–Verlag, 1980.

3. Haynes, H., White, B. L. and Held, R. 'Visual accommodation in human infants.' *Science*, 1965, **148**, 528–530.
4. Sander, L. W., Stechler, G., Burns, P. and Burns, J. H. 'Early mother–infant interaction and 24-hour patterns of activity and sleep.' *J. Amer. Acad. Child Psychiat.*, 1970, **9** 103–123.

5   Life with infants

1. Laslett, P. *The World We Have Lost.* London: Methuen, 1971.
2. Rapoport, R., Rapoport, R. N. and Strelitz, Z. *Fathers, Mothers and Others.* London: Routledge and Kegan Paul, 1977.
3. Clarke, A. M. and Clarke, A. D. B. *Early Experience. Myth and Evidence.* London: Open Books, 1976.
4. Wollheim, R. *Freud.* London: Fontana/Collins, 1971.
5. Rich, A. *Of Women Born: Motherhood as Experience and Institution.* London: Virago, 1976.
   Oakley, A. *Becoming a Mother.* Oxford: Martin Robinson, 1979.
6. Cartwright, A. *The Dignity of Labour?* London: Tavistock, 1979.
7. Brown, G. W. and Harris, T. *Social Origins of Depression.* London: Tavistock, 1978.
8. Rutter, M. *Maternal Deprivation Reassessed.* London: Penguin, 1972.
9. Kempe, R. S. and Kempe, C. H. *Child Abuse.* London: Open Books/Fontana, 1978.

6   Communication and games

1. Lock, A. (Ed.). *Action, Gesture and Symbol: the emergence of language.* London/NY: Academic Press, 1978.
2. MacMurray, J. *Persons in Relation.* London: Faber and Faber, 1970.
3. Stern, D. *The First Relationship: Infant and Mother.* London: Open Books, 1977.
4. Richards, M. P. M. 'Social interaction in the first weeks of human life.' *Psychiat. Neurol. Neurochir.*, 1971, **14**, 35–42.
5. Richards, M. P. M. (Ed.). *The Integration of a Child into a Social World.* London: Cambridge University Press, 1974.
6. Becker, E. *The Birth and Death of Meaning.* London: Penguin, 1972.

7   Girls and boys: fathers and mothers

1. Mead, M. *Male and Female.* London: Penguin, 1962.
2. Hutt, C. *Males and Females.* London: Penguin, 1972.
3. Maccoby, M. M. and Jacklin, C. N. *The Psychology of Sex Differences.* Stanford: Stanford University Press, 1974.
4. Richards, M. P. M., Bernal, J. F. and Brackbill, Y. 'Early Behavioural Differences: Gender or Circumcision?' *Developm. Psychobiology*, 1976, **9**, 89–95.
5. Money, J. and Ehrhardt, A. A. *Man and Woman, boy and girl.* Baltimore: Johns Hopkins University Press, 1972.
6. Lamb, M. E. (Ed.). *The Role of the Father in Child Development.* NY/London: John Wiley, 1976.

8   Learning to move and learning to think

1. Zelazo, N. A., Zelazo, P. R. and Kolb, S. 'Walking in the newborn.' *Science*, 1972, **176**, 314–315.
2. McGraw, M. B. *Growth: A Study of Johnny and Jimmy.* NY: Appleton-Century-Croft, 1935.

3. Piaget, J. *Origins of Intelligence in the Child*. London: Routledge and Kegan Paul, 1953.
4. Donaldson, M. *Children's Minds*. London: Fontana/Collins, 1978.
5. Hunt, J. McV. *Intelligence and Experience*. NY: Ronald Press, 1961.

9   The end of infancy
1. Lyons, J. *Chomsky*. London: Fontana/Collins, 1976.
2. Bates, E. *Language and context. The Acquisition of pragmatics*. NY/London: Academic Press, 1976.
3. Snow, C. E. 'Mother's speech to children learning language.' *Child Developm.*, 1972, **43**, 549–565.
4. Bloom, L. M. *One Word at a Time*. The Hague: Mouton, 1973.
5. Brown, R. *A First Language. The early stages*. Cambridge, Mass.: Harvard University Press, 1973.
6. Vygotsky, L. S. *Thought and Language*. NY: Wiley, 1962.

Index

Photo credits

Yael Braun—13 (*bottom*); Bob Bray—27, 35, 38, 39, 52, 54 (*4*), 77, 87, 89 (*left*), 106, 117; Ron Chapman—83; Chusak—41 (*top*); Ronald Cohen—24, 40 (*top*); Creativ Color A/S (courtesy of Lego)—109 (*top*); John Garrett—12, 13 (*top*), 16 (*2*), 36, 41 (*bottom*), 44 (*2*), 45 (*2*), 53, 68 (*top*), 69, 80, 101, 109 (*bottom*), 112; Geoslides—40 (*bottom*); Henry Grant—73; Greenhill—5, 7 (*4*), 70, 72 (*bottom*), 86, 88, 102, 119; Yaacov Harlap—10, 29, 42 (*middle*); Simon Harper—76 (*2*), 97; Kristal—68 (*bottom*), 105; Sheelah Latham—110; Leimbach—25, 85; Lisa Mackson—33, 37 (*top*); R. Milon—42 (*right*); Margaret Murray—122; PAF—82, 120; Rex Features—8, 9, 19, 23 (*3*), 37 (*bottom*), 47, 48, 56 (*2*), 60, 61, 66, 72 (*top*), 92, 103 (*bottom*), 104, 108, 115, (CML Studios Ltd.) 55, (David W. Corson from A. Devaney, N.Y.) 51 (*6*), 103 (*top*), (Herrmann) 89 (*right*), 98, (Hannes Kilian) 46 (*2*), (David McEnery) 123, (Pierluigi Picture Feature Services) 11, (Spillman & Ramsay) 42 (*left*); Len Rhodes—65, Anthea Sieveking—14, 71, 91; Homer Sykes—84.

Illustrator Malcolm Ward (Youe & Spooner)—57.

Multimedia Publications Inc have endeavoured to observe the legal requirements with regard to the rights of the suppliers of graphic and photographic materials.